Happiness Is Growing a Marriage

Happiness Is
Growing a Marriage

©VOLK

Published for the ALDERSGATE ASSOCIATES
By Beacon Hill Press of Kansas City
Kansas City, Missouri

ALDERSGATE

Gene Van Note
Editor

Mabeth Clem
Editorial Assistant

ISBN: 0-8341-0703-1

Cover Photo: H. Armstrong Roberts

Photos: 7—Figge; 13, 97—A. Devaney, Inc.; 20, 105—Dave Anderson; 27—Jim Whit-mer; 37, 45, 52—H. Armstrong Roberts; 60, 69—Camerique; 76—Rising Hope; 86—De Wys, Inc.

Contents

Chapter 1

Happiness Is a Growing Marriage

by O'Neal Weeks

Background Scriptures:
Colossians 2:6-7; Ephesians 3:16-21

Time was when happiness *(marital happiness, at least)* was a stable, static marriage in which the partners played their roles well: the husband as provider, authority, disciplinarian; the wife as housekeeper, ego-supporter for husband, and child-bearer and nurturer.

Then came industrialization, urbanization, mechanization, mobilization, and impersonalization. Families moved away from relatives into towns and cities where they lived among strangers and worked with people they did not know. Extended kin interactions were minimized. All this made the primary family—husband, wife, and, in some cases, children—the major source of happiness.

The emphasis in family-related values shifted from stability to happiness as the primary value. This change, accompanied by an increasingly romantic perception of marriage, led to the popular *and-they-lived-happily-ever-after* myth. And a myth it is! Research reveals what many married couples have known for a long time: there is a great deal of disenchantment with marriage.

The promise of marital bliss is broken as ecstasy gives way to the strains of responsibility, more realistic perception of one's partner, the monotony of routines, and conflict. What promised to be a dynamic, vital relationship becomes devitalized and dull. The marriage stagnates and deteriorates until it is at best only tolerated.

But it does not have to be that way, as many couples are

discovering. Marriage can be a dynamic, vital, growing relationship.

One thing that prevents growth in a marriage relationship is the myth of *romanticism.* This is the idealization of marriage and of the marriage partner. This is a part of the *love-is-blind syndrome,* and it involves a response to either a partial or distorted love object. This kind of love sees only what it wants or needs to see in the beloved.

This kind of idealized image cannot survive in an intimate relationship. One of three things will happen: (1) intimacy will be lost in attempts to maintain one's projected self-image or facade and his idealistic, distorted image of his partner; (2) the distorted images will give way to reality, resulting in disillusionment, disenchantment, disappointment, and deterioration; or (3) images will be dropped, the partners will get in touch with their own and each other's true selves, and they will develop a growing intimacy in their relationship.

Dishonesty and *lack of openness* with each other also hinder growth. For a relationship to grow, it is essential that the persons involved really know and understand each other. They must learn to share their hurts, anger, doubts, frustrations, joys—their whole range of feelings. To the extent that you keep feelings—positive or negative—hidden inside you, you keep your partner at a distance. That prevents growth.

Some happiness techniques (such as those advocated in popular books like *The Total Woman*) are designed to deceive, manipulate, cover feelings, or satisfy the needs of one partner at the expense of the other. Games like these produce only superficial happiness at the expense of more in-depth growth. Such happiness fades when the players tire of the game.

Growth in marriage is also discouraged by a *role-based relationship*—a relationship in which each partner has a rigidly defined set of roles and most of their interaction focuses on their role-functioning. A woman who is a very good wife and mother may be married to a man who is a very good husband and father (they perform well in those roles), but *their* relationship may be so set in concrete that it cannot grow.

Another thing that hinders the growth of a marriage is

emphasizing the parent-child relationship to the neglect of the husband-wife relationship. The parent-child relationship is very important, but it should not take priority over the marital relationship.

The first child is born to many couples within a year after the wedding. For the next two decades the marriage is placed in limbo as the parents focus most of their interests and energy on the children. Then they wake up one day 20 or 25 years later and realize the children are gone and they still have two or three decades of marriage left. They rush to reclaim their relationship, only to find there's nothing left to reclaim. Then they are faced with loneliness and disillusionment. If a marriage is to grow, it must be cultivated during the child-bearing days.

So much for some of the barriers to marital growth. How can you develop your marriage into a growing thing or cultivate the growth that is already there?

First, honestly assess where you are in your marriage now. This should be done with your partner, preferably when you have some leisurely, unhurried time together. You may want to do some private assessing, and then evaluate your marriage together. Here are some points on which you might focus. You will probably think of others.

What is the status of love in your relationship? How rapidly your pulse beats or how restricted your breathing becomes or how flushed you feel when you touch is not what's important here. But what are some of the deeper feelings you have for your spouse?

One psychologist has said that love exists when another's needs, security, and sense of well-being become as important to you as your own. Another says that to love a person is to grant him the full right to his unique personhood, and to affirm him as a person. Still another writes of love as an activity involving knowledge, responsibility, respect, and care. Real love is more than passion.

To love another person involves respecting and caring about yourself and your own needs. Loving another person does not mean making his needs and his satisfaction *more* important than yours but *as* important. Didn't Jesus say that the way to love another is to love him *as* you love yourself? No more, no less.

How committed are you to caring for and meeting the needs of your spouse? How committed is he or she to meeting yours? You must be open and honest with each other regarding your needs and expectations. Do not assume you know what your spouse needs or expects from you, no matter how well you know him. Ask him. Let your spouse know how well he is meeting your needs—and which ones are not being met. Gentle candor is essential.

What are the strengths and weaknesses of your marriage? What do you find satisfying about your marriage? What about it bothers or disappoints you? Be very honest. Be very specific. This exercise can get lost in generalizations. Discuss what can be done about the things that bother you. What are some strengths you have on which to build?

Where is your marriage now as compared to 1, 5, or 10 years ago? Is it where you had hoped it would be now? Has it grown? Stagnated? Deteriorated?

At what specific points would you like to see growth in your marriage? What will it take? What are some changes *you* are willing to make to accomplish growth in your relationship?

After evaluating the present status of your marriage, the next step is to set growth goals for your relationship. Where would you like your marriage to be one year and five years from now? Talk about specific expectations and goals both of you have. What specific actions must you take *now* to help insure the realization of those goals? Are you willing to act on these?

Finally, both partners need to commit themselves to work at developing the skills needed to maintain growth in their marriage.

Learn to share your feelings with your partner. This will involve self-awareness, getting in touch with your own feelings. Many of us have become so accustomed to suppressing feelings that we are not aware of them. Let yourself experience your emotions—then share them, as you experience them, with your partner. Sharing feelings with each other leads to growth and greater intimacy.

Develop a good style of communication. Learn to say exactly what you mean. Do not assume you know what your partner is thinking. Learn to ask. Listen to what your partner says. Then check it out for clarification before drawing conclusions.

Learn to handle conflict constructively. Conflict is a normal, healthy part of a growing relationship. Conflict, constructively handled, never hurts a relationship. It can even help it to grow. Learn to fight fair, attacking issues rather than each other. Be sensitive to the things you fight about because these are good clues to growth. They should help you identify what it will take to improve your marriage.

These suggestions are too brief to be considered an adequate do-it-yourself guide to marital growth. If there are serious problems in your relationship, you should not attempt to carry out these suggestions without the assistance of someone skilled and trained in marital counseling. Many pastors are trained marriage counselors.

You are not alone in your struggle for growth in marriage. In fact, many couples these days are participating in marriage enrichment seminars and workshops. In these conferences, couples join together under the leadership of a trained person to learn how to communicate more effectively, how to deal constructively with conflict, and how to give each other support in relationship. Many churches are now offering such group experiences for couples.

Whether a couple shares the inspiration of an enrichment retreat or experiments with new relationships privately, the key is this: happiness is a growing marriage.

From *Home Life,* January 1977. © Copyright 1976 The Sunday School Board of the Southern Baptist Convention. All rights reserved. Used by permission.

Chapter 2

This Is Where I Am—
Where Are You?

by Colleen Townsend Evans and
Louis H. Evans, Jr.

Background Scriptures:
Psalm 34:3; Ephesians 5:19-20, 33; Colossians 3:19

It was Sunday . . . a beautiful spring evening in the hills of Bel Air, Calif. The scent of night-blooming jasmine came through the open windows on the wings of a gentle breeze, and it seemed that all was well with the world.

I was getting ready for the evening service of the new church Louie had been sent to Bel Air to start. I was standing in front of the big mirror in our bathroom, brushing my hair. I remember hearing the front door open and close as people began to congregate in our living room as they did each Sunday night. Louie had been out making calls on new members, and now I heard him open the sliding glass door into our bedroom—no doubt slipping in the back way so he could catch his breath and wash up before facing nearly 100 people sitting in our front room.

Our life since arriving at Bel Air had been a fast track— I mean, *really!* . . . A constant round of calls, meetings, and people. It wasn't that we were never together—just so rarely *alone.* It had been weeks since we had an evening to ourselves. I was tired. We had four babies under five years of age, and a home that doubled as a church office, sanctuary, and fellowship hall. But more than being tired, I was in some strange way lonely. Not that I didn't love our work. I was as excited about it as Louie was . . . and our people were marvelous. But something was wrong, and I was just beginning to wrestle with whatever it was.

At that point, enter Louie. There he was, standing beside me, washing his hands. He was excited about the call he had just made, thrilled with what God was doing in the lives of peo-

ple in our fellowship, and eagerly planning the next project to move on to in the church—and the next, and the next.

Now, at that point, as the good wife, I of course shared his enthusiasm—right? Wrong! The more he talked and the more excited he became, the more I grappled with my churning insides. My feelings rose higher and higher, that lump in my throat got bigger, and finally the tears spilled over the top, and I let him have it. Poor Louie! All those people in the living room waiting to be inspired, and his wife dissolves in tears in the bathroom. But he listened, and I'll always be grateful to him for that.

I'm not sure exactly what I said, but between sniffs and sobs I was somehow able to tell Louie about the need I was just beginning to sense within myself. I told him how hungry I was to be with him, to have time to talk and dream, alone. I shared my strong feeling that there had to be a change in our relentless schedule, a change that would give us time to communicate and build our relationship.

Well, there obviously wasn't time for Louie to hear me out completely just then, but later—after the meeting was over and the door had closed for the last time—he did. We sat and talked for a very long time, saying things we both wanted and needed to hear—things we had been almost too busy to think, much less say to one another. I remember Louie thanked me for being honest about my feelings—and that meant something special to me. He also agreed that indeed we did need to slow down in order to have time to nurture our own relationship.

And then he did a simple, practical—and, to me, very beautiful—thing. He took his little date book from his pocket, and looked until he found a free night. It happened to be Thursday of the following week, and he said, "That's our night." And so it was the next week that we had an evening all to ourselves. Out of that night came a decision to put aside time every week for the same purpose . . . and so it has been in all the years since . . . Thursday night.

Now I'm sure many couples are able to *find* time for each other in an easy, unscheduled way, and that's wonderful. But that didn't work for us. With our kind of life we found we had to *make* time—not that we would always be able to adhere to it rigidly—literally grabbing hold of our schedules and writing it into our date books. And that was one of the most important decisions we ever made . . . the decision to *make* time to say, "This is where I am; where are you?" Any marriage, or any relationship of depth, will only be as good as its communication. And communication takes time!

It also takes being *aware* of where you are, for communication is not just talking *to,* or *at* someone. It is a sharing of real feelings . . . what we think, feel, value—what we fear, hate—what we dream about and believe in.

Communication is part of being an authentic person . . . we say what we feel and feel what we say. Of course, we do not communicate only through our words. We communicate in many different ways at the same time, so that even the sharing of a few words can send a very complicated message. In fact, whether we speak or not, in an intimate relationship we are constantly sending and receiving messages. We can speak volumes with a look, a tone of voice, a touch on the shoulder as we pass our partner's chair at the family table. A person who truly communicates will "match" inside and out. As we grow in our ability to communicate in marriage we can help each other to become authentic people—we can know ourselves better and match inside and out. In a way, I must be able to share who I am transparently with my husband in order to *know* who I am.

The cry for communication is loud and persistent! Among the women I know, I hear this hunger expressed more than any other: "If only my husband would talk to me!" "We just *don't* communicate." Or, "He's so busy making money! I don't want his money, I want *him!*"

Women are hungry for their men . . . hungry to know and be known. But it doesn't go only one way. Men, too, have this basic desire, and how healthy it is that our society is finally granting its permission for men to express their needs openly. The drive we feel to know and be known is not linked to our sex, but to our basic humanity. We want it so much because God created us to have it.

15

In working through problems and conflicts there are some steps, or dynamics, of communication that can be helpful. Because they have worked for people we know—and for us— I would like to share them in the hope that they will be useful to someone else in a time of need. I like them, not because they are foolproof (they're not), but because they offer partners the opportunity to minister to one another in the process.

First, if one partner is really troubled by a problem or situation, the other partner has to resist counterattacking and just hold his tongue for a while. That does not mean he becomes a doormat or a target for abuse. Perhaps for a short time he has to be dumped on, but the important thing is that he gives the other person a chance to unburden himself.

The listener in this case is the minister to the other. Sometimes he may have to try to extract whatever it is that has built up inside the other. Perhaps a husband needs to communicate that he's having a painfully hard time with his boss. Perhaps a wife is troubled by an interfering mother, or she may be having problems with *her* boss. Maybe something in their relationship is painful. Whatever it is, it has to come out, and it never will if both partners are wounding each other with their angry barbs.

When the listening partner feels that the other has finally gotten it all out, that's the time for him to go back over the same ground, asking, "Is this how you feel? Am I getting it right?" He is not agreeing with the other person; he is trying to determine where the other person is. Perhaps the other partner will have to correct him a few times, but finally the listener should be able to say, "Yes, I understand."

Second, now that the dark river has begun to dissipate, the clear stream of insight can begin to flow. The listener continues to listen, giving the other partner the freedom to explore the causes and sources of his anger. It's important for the listener to refrain from making any suggestions of his own. Let the other person identify his own problems, difficult and halting as that may be.

Third, once a partner knows what is bothering him, he can begin to consider alternative solutions. Again, the listening

16

partner shouldn't try to impose answers on him, although he can help to explore the solutions open to the other person. If a boss is domineering, or if a mother is the kind who tries to tell a wife how to bring up her children, what can the other person do about it? And what might the outcome be? Perhaps these same alternatives occurred to the troubled person earlier, but because he couldn't articulate them they seemed too risky. Now that he is able to talk about them with an understanding listener, they may seem totally different to him. Perhaps a husband will decide that he wants to change his job. Or he may decide that he can handle his anger without taking it out on his wife. Perhaps a wife may decide that there is a way she can encounter her mother without destroying the relationship. And at this point perhaps one partner may be able to say to the other, "Honey, just the fact that I'm talking this out with you makes me feel better."

Fourth, any decision made immediately after an outburst of anger should be reconsidered later. Sometimes, in the wake of an emotional explosion, a person is so eager to compromise that he may regret his decision later. So, after a day or two, the listening partner should talk over the decision with him, asking, "Is this what you meant? Is this what we agreed to do?" If the other person has second thoughts, the decision should be altered to include them.

Fifth, okay—each partner knows how the troubled one is going to deal with the source of his anger. What then? Is the problem solved? Will there never be another outburst over this same issue? Not on your life! Here is where the ministering partner must be *patient* and *prayerful* . . . two of the best ways to support the one he loves.

Usually problems are caused by deep habit patterns. If we human beings were able to change direction on a dime, our lives would be so different. But because many of our responses are conditioned over long periods of time, our old habits usually linger for a while after we begin asking God to break us free of them. As Corrie ten Boom says, "After you stop ringing a bell, there may be a few *dings* left." No matter how vehemently one partner proclaims that he is going to change his behavior,

17

there's the chance he'll get into the same rut again—possibly again and again.

What does the ministering partner do when that happens? Does he say, "You dope! You blew it!"? Not if he has faith in the other person's potential. Instead of making the other partner feel like a failure because he goofed, the ministering partner says, "Hey, I'm hanging in there with you. I know it's tough, but I'm praying with you, and with God's help, I know you can do it." And when the day comes that the old response gives way to a new one, no one is more grateful than the ministering partner.

This process of communication is one more way of submitting to one another out of reverence for Christ . . . submitting to the need of one partner to be heard and understood. In the last 25 years Louie has submitted to me many times—and I to him—in this way. We don't take turns or keep score. It happens when it needs to happen. It takes time, emotional energy, and patience on the part of the listener, but the reward of SHALOM (the real peace that comes after struggle) is worth it all. As one couple who have grown in their ability to share deeply put it: "Now we can talk as two human beings instead of paper dolls labeled 'wife' and 'husband.'"

Communication is work; it is costly; but it is one of the best investments any of us who are married can make.

Excerpted from *My Lover, My Friend*, by Colleen Townsend Evans and Louis H. Evans, Jr. Copyright © 1976 by Fleming H. Revell Company. Used by permission.

Chapter 3

Choosing
Constructive Conflict

by Carole Mayhall

Background Scriptures:
Philippians 4:4-8; Ephesians 4:26-27

A value tag is attached to depth in communication: it is definitely worth the cost! The price is exacted in *time* (with the TV set turned off, getting up a bit earlier in the morning, a little less sleep at night when something needs to be discussed at length) and in *vulnerability.*

Many couples discover a tension-filled topic in their first year of marriage and bury it hastily for fear of creating problems. The second year another major issue surfaces, so they dig a grave for that one too. By year five, they are simply not talking about anything except surface issues. The silence screams, "Something is wrong," and all those buried conflicts grow increasingly rotten till the stench cannot be tolerated. Something is dead . . . and it could be the marriage.

Silence in a marriage may denote fear, a lack of caring what the other partner thinks, or an unwillingness to pay the price of deep sharing.

But silence isn't the only wall we have to overcome. Elmer and Sue set up a number of unconscious communication hurdles which caused them both to fall frequently in the dust.

1. *Too Busy*—One evening Sue said, "Elmer, I'd like to talk with you about something that has been bothering me lately."

Elmer responded, "Not now, Sue. There's a football game on TV and I want to watch it. Let's talk about it later."

But somehow after dinner he had business that had to be taken care of and an important telephone call to make. After that he was just too tired. He had effectively blocked all real communication by being "too busy."

2. *Changing the Subject*—Two weeks later Elmer came home discouraged and upset. He had been wrestling with some

personnel problems at work and wanted to talk about them with his wife. Just as he got the conversation started, Sue interrupted, "Honey, did you remember to pay the water bill yesterday?"

She had effectively indicated to him that she was not interested in his problems at work. (Later she complained that he never discussed his job with her.)

3. *Defensiveness*—So Elmer carried his problems alone. But the personnel problems did not dissolve and he became irritable. One night he tried to reach Sue again and said, "Sue, you don't seem very interested in my problems at work."

In quick succession she looked stricken, hurt, and finally angry. She exploded, "You don't think so? Well, you don't listen to me either! How many times have I tried to tell you something and you kept right on reading your paper? Don't talk to me about not listening."

Defensiveness blocks necessary communication, yet we all practice it so successfully. It is the opposite of the biblical injunction to "walk in love and wisdom" (see Ephesians 5:2, 15).

Sue needed God's grace to respond with, "You're right, Elmer. I'm sorry. Tell me what I can do and how I can help you. I really will try to be a better listener and I am interested in your problems. Please forgive me." But she didn't do it.

4a. *Super Guilt*—Sue's defensiveness caused Elmer to drop the subject and grow more silent and depressed. A week later Sue said, "Elmer, you have spent only 15 minutes with the kids this week, and even less with me. I really feel the need for more of your time."

Elmer responded, "You are absolutely right. I am the world's worst father and husband. I don't know how you put up with me. I am a total failure."

What could Sue say? He really wasn't *that* bad. So she reassured him and dropped the subject. Elmer had effectively blocked any in-depth talking by his expression of super-guilt. Dr. James Mallory of the Atlanta Christian Counseling Center has suggested that those who act or feel *this* guilty have no intention of changing, because if they did, they would not need to feel so guilty.[1]

4b. *Peace at Any Price*—A variation of the super-guilt attitude is the "peace at any price" giving-in person. Some husbands have abdicated their leadership in the family and gone down to defeat by this method. Content with exercising control at their office or job, their constant response at home is, "Do whatever you want to. You decide." This tactic makes the wife feel alone and insecure. Eventually this attitude leads to such repressed feelings of frustration in both husband and wife that joy is gone from their relationship and their communion is crushed.

5. *Rejection of Feelings*—Two days later Elmer said to Sue, "You know, I really am feeling like a failure in my work and as a husband and father. I feel very ineffective in my life right now."

He was finally being honest and vulnerable. But Sue responded, "Oh, you shouldn't feel that way. It's dumb for you to feel that way."

The major problem was that Elmer *did* feel exactly that way. And all Sue's protests would not change the way he felt. Dr. Mallory writes:

> This disallowance of feeling, just because you don't happen to agree, is a very common block in communication. When you shoot back, "It's dumb to feel that way," or "How can you feel that way?" you are in fact hitting at the very core of the person. It represents a denunciation or belittlement. Rightly or wrongly the person has those feelings. They are part of him. Disallowing feelings is a deep rejection of the person himself. Instead, we should try to understand the person's feelings. This encourages communication and assists us to be helpful.[2]

Sue rejected Elmer's feelings about himself because they threatened her security in his job and in their relationship. But her rejection made him pull back further into his silence, trying to handle his frustrations by himself. His inadequacies had actually been reinforced by Sue's response.

Jack and I are learning that we must get things out in the open—to be real with each other, to share feelings and needs and desires. There are times, of course, when the best course is to end a discussion temporarily. Sometimes I have to quit because tears make it impossible for me to say more. At other times the edge of my anger is too sharp to risk saying anything because I know I may get destructive. But we must never withdraw permanently. We must come back to the issue at hand and resolve it or there will be untold consequences. But how in the world should we handle anger?

In a book I read, the author said that if you can handle anger positively by giving several positive statements to one negative statement, you should "give yourself a kiss." If you blew up and spouted out all your anger with venom and hostility, you should still "give yourself a kiss" because you have expressed your anger verbally rather than expressing it in other hostile ways which would have been more destructive.

It may be true that to express anger verbally is better than having an ulcer, or becoming frigid, dejected, or depressed. But instead of ventilating all the time, we need to turn to the Word of God. The Lord has a far better way for us to handle anger.

In studying God's ways of handling conflicts, Jack and I find these principles helpful for married couples to "have a really *good* fight," that is, to have a creative conflict under God's rules.

1. *Keep Cool!*—The Bible says that "a quick-tempered man acts foolishly" (Proverbs 14:17, NASB),* and "a hot-tempered man stirs up strife, / But the slow to anger pacifies contention" (15:18). God's Word further states that a man with a "cool spirit" is one with understanding (17:27-28). *That's* the kind of understanding we need.

Many factors help us in staying cool. Practicing thinking before we speak and learning to handle conflicts lovingly and without rancor are two of the most important. "The heart of the righteous ponders how to answer" (15:28), Solomon said, and "where there are many words, transgression is unavoidable, / But he who restrains his lips is wise" (10:19).

In order to stay cool and not get angry or overly emotional, we may need to back away from the conflict for a time. "The beginning of strife is like letting out water, / So abandon the quarrel before it breaks out" (17:14). This does not mean abandoning the *conflict* or working through to a solution, but when it becomes angry quarreling (or just before), leave it for a while. Come back to it after praying and thinking about it.

2. *Make Understanding Your Aim*—The aim in many of our conflicts seems to be to vent our anger and feelings at the other person. Solomon says, "A fool does not delight in understanding, / But only in revealing his own mind" (18:2). In order to understand, we have to *listen* and hear the other person completely ("He who gives an answer before he hears, / It is folly and shame to him" [18:13]), and *try to see* the issue from the other's point of view.

So often we *presume* we know the facts and feelings of the other person. Yet "through *presumption* comes nothing but strife" (13:10, italics added). A conflict cannot be entered with the idea that one must "win." There is no winning or losing in a *good* conflict, but a breaking through to better understanding of each other. Otherwise you have both lost. When one person in a marital relationship is determined to win, *both* really lose because they have lost understanding and unity.

3. *Keep Short Accounts*—The Bible says that we are not to let the sun go down on our anger (Ephesians 4:26). This means that the deadline for solving a problem of anger and breaking through to a better understanding is the last time we see that person *that* day. For husbands and wives that would be bedtime; for conflicts at work sunset would be quitting time.

4. *Act Wisely, Not Foolishly*—God says it is a foolish man who either gets angry or makes light of the other person's feelings or point of view. "When a wise man has a controversy with a foolish man, / The foolish man either rages or laughs, and there is no rest" (Proverbs 29:9). Solomon also says, "A fool always loses his temper, / But a wise man holds it back" (29:11).

A wise person will not block the flow of God through his or her life with big chunks of self. God needs to control us in times of conflict as much as in times of calm. For His control at all times in our lives, we must practice Solomon's words of advice, "Do not let kindness and truth leave you; / Bind them around your neck, / Write them on the tablet of your heart. / So you will find favor and good repute / In the sight of God and man. / Trust in the Lord with all your heart, / And do not lean on your own understanding. / In all your ways acknowledge Him, / And He will make your paths straight" (3:3-6).

The following are ways in which you can do so: (1) be kind, truthful, and trusting that God will lead you; (2) do not be wise in your own eyes; (3) ask God to make you a wise person and remember that a wise person accepts correction (see 9:8); and (4) be aware of the tone of your voice. Try lowering it instead of raising it by remembering that "a gentle answer turns away wrath, / But a harsh word stirs up anger" (15:1).

In handling their conflicts, Elmer and Sue have some learning to do and so do we. Being too busy to talk, half listening, defensiveness, and the disallowing of the other's feelings—all these must be considered. We must take a stand for open and free discussion, allowing feelings to be expressed. Depth, sharing, and openness can be fully experienced as we grow in our knowledge of God and of one another.

1. James D. Mallory, Jr., *The Kink and I* (Wheaton, III.: Victor Books, 1973), p. 22.
2. Ibid., p. 19.

Chapter 11 of *Marriage Takes More than Love,* by Jack and Carole Mayhall, © 1978 by The Navigators (NavPress, Colorado Springs, CO 80901). Used by permission.

*All scripture quotations in this chapter are from the *New American Standard Bible* (NASB), © The Lockman Foundation, 1960, 1962, 1968, 1971, 1972, 1973, 1975, and are used by permission.

Chapter 4

"I" and "You" Messages

by James G. T. Fairfield

Background Scriptures: Psalm 19:14; Proverbs 12: 17-18, 22; 14:29; 15:1, 4; 16:32; 18:21; 19:20; 21:23; 25:21

"Jed was mad at me for something," Colleen explained. "It was more than just some little thing, but I couldn't understand what was bugging him. When I asked him to tell me what was wrong, he said nothing was wrong at all.

"But there was; I could tell. He had a quietness about him, you know? A person can feel it when someone else is holding back. We just weren't having the easy time together we'd been having. Instead, Jed was getting quieter and more like he didn't want to talk except about ordinary things, like where he'd put his car keys.

"It got so bad one weekend I couldn't take it any longer. He said something, nothing really, and I started to cry—I couldn't help it. He started to go out, and I wouldn't let him. I stood in front of the door and told him he'd have to hurt me to move me and I wanted to know what it was I'd done or was doing that he didn't like."

Colleen finally got to the point of confronting Jed—let's heave a sigh of relief! Now we'll hear from Jed.

"I shouldn't have let it build up in me, but for a while I hardly knew what it was that bugged me. By the time I figured it out, I was just plain ornery enough to figure she kept doing it to make me sore.

"I'd pick her up at her job on the way home from work bone tired, but she'd run her mouth about all the flak she got from customers. Some days all the way home. All through supper. One nonstop gripe. It got on my nerves."

Let's look at Jed-the-sullen and his problem.

1. Isn't he being an irrational slob? To blame her for doing it to make him angry?

2. Just like most of us, Jed let himself build a little irritation into a mountain of rejection.

3. Why didn't he confront Colleen with his need to back off from the pressures of the day and talk small talk while he unwound?

4. And if he couldn't offer sympathy, why didn't he challenge Colleen's gripes in a way that might help her survive the customer flak without pulling him down?

But such is the stuff of broken relationships. Little straws of hostility that build up a backbreaking load of antipathies and antagonisms. Now let's see how confronting might have worked.

Colleen does finally confront Jed with a last-ditch stand at the front door. As mean and miserable as they both feel at that moment, it's even money Colleen will pick up a fat lip and Jed a scratched eye. But supposing Jed catches the hurt in her tears and the desperation in her voice? She is asking for openness from Jed. She risks being hurt more if Jed ignores her or evades the question.

Worse, he could pretend as he has been doing that there's nothing wrong. He could cover up and tell her he loves her, ask why she's getting upset over nothing. But that would be patching a growing wound with a Band-Aid of false and momentary warmth.

A lot of us do that sort of thing. We avoid: "Surely you're kidding, Colleen—what's for supper?"

Or we placate: "I'm sorry. Have I been making you feel bad? What a terrible thing to do!" Recognize the YIELD strategy? Or we shout the other person down in true WIN style. "You're out of your skull, woman. Shut up and let me out the door before I deck you."

But the need here is for Jed to level with Colleen. She has invited an honest, clear statement like this from Jed: "I'm tired when I pick you up from work and then I get a load of grief from your job dumped on me that I haven't the strength or the inclination right then to handle."

He's saying what he feels. He's still blaming her a little and there's a disguised "you dump a load on me every day" which blames her for his anger. It would have been better to explain: "I'm tired when I pick you up and I don't like the struggle right then of dealing with tensions I feel from your job."

That's an "I message" which is considerably different in effect from a "you message." "You messages" throw the burden of the whole problem back on the other person. "You start griping about your work as soon as you get in the car. You make me angry." Or "Why can't you handle your own job and its problems? Why do you dump them on me?"

"You messages" obscure the underlying causes of conflict. When I blame *you* for my anger, then I'm saying, "Your action caused my anger. Now you must act to make me feel right again."

In effect I give you power over my reactions and I will hold my anger toward you until you meet my demands. I give you power to please me or to keep me angry and I am powerless to deal with my own reactions. I must wait on you to ease my anger. I am unable to be me, and by imposing on you the burden of healing my hurts, I won't let you be yourself either.

But if I recognize that *I* make me angry, then what you do does not control my reaction. I am responsible for my perceptions and feelings and what I will do about them.

"I messages" help clear the air as to who owns the problem. Jed blamed his anger on Colleen, but Jed could have reacted with sympathy; so his brooding anger was *his* problem.

Let's look at another couple. Perry and Wilma, in their mid-40s, with children 19, 16, and 15. The oldest and youngest seemed normal and well-adjusted, but 16-year-old Bruce gave them fits. According to Wilma, the boy left his room in a mess, wouldn't take a bath every day, and ignored her when she spoke to him about it. On the other hand, Bruce insisted his room suited him fine, and he saw no reason to shower every day. "I'll shrink with all the wrinkles," he said.

Wilma badgered Perry to correct the boy, insisting that

her husband stand with her. Perry attempted to discipline Bruce, even helped him to clean up his room. Wilma objected to this as letting the boy get away with his rebelliousness. At this point Perry defended Bruce as "just going through a phase" and a serious quarrel erupted.

Whose problem is this? Bruce doesn't seem to have had any to begin with, although he certainly has one now with a fight going between his parents over his conduct.

Perry didn't have a problem with Bruce's messiness until he (1) took up Wilma's cause and attempted to correct Bruce and (2) then failed to satisfy Wilma's demand.

Wilma had the problem to begin with. She didn't like the mess. ("I have to clean this house, you know.") She didn't like a break in the routine of daily baths she had long assumed were next to godliness. She had attempted to make her problem Perry's as well as Bruce's. When Bruce refused to accept her standard any longer, she turned it on her husband. When he vacillated she felt she must stand her ground and get things straight with Perry and with her son.

Now let's try to help Wilma identify her feelings. We can make an educated guess as to what her underlying reactions are to Bruce's behavior. If she could think them through, she might come up with these.

1. Like a lot of us, Wilma has learned that neatness is a helpful discipline. She feels Bruce's character would benefit by that kind of self-control.

2. Wilma knows how many allergens and bugs can blossom in the "dust bunnies" a messy room can breed. She fears for Bruce's health, and for the overall health of her family.

3. When she vacuums the rest of the house, she expects to face a certain amount of disarray. But not this disaster!

4. She gets steamed at having to clean up after this hulking litterbug. "He's 16, not in diapers!"

5. She feels put-upon by her son, having to be his slave, garbage man, and valet.

Six, seven, eight, etc., are vague fears that she is raising a delinquent bum who will disgrace her and bring humiliation upon them all.

But does she explain these to Bruce? No. Instead she demands "for the 50th time" that her son clean up his room. She nags him. She reminds him he is personally unkempt. She tells him he's a menace to them all.

She nags Perry, rides his back to whip his son into line: "Can't you do something with that boy?" When he fails, she turns her frustrations full on Perry and the battle is on, folks.

But suppose she were to confront Bruce, on her own, like this:

"It's a real drag to have to clean up your room, Bruce. It's hard work—and I want to get rid of the dust and dead bugs so you—or one of the rest of us—won't come down with something."

With some children an appeal to hygiene or logic simply won't do the trick. They need the stronger confrontation of the personal effect of their actions. Perhaps something like this: "I like my job usually. I like organizing a house to run smoothly, and I feel responsible to keep it going that way; so when I bump into a frustration like I feel with the mess in your room—well, I'm frustrated, for sure!"

These are "I messages." Wilma talks about the situation in terms of how it affects her. She expresses *her* needs, without nagging or name-calling.

Bruce may respond by cleaning up his room, because he hears the underlying reasons for his mother's concerns in a way that doesn't coerce his response. But what if he just comes back with more of the "Aw, Mom, you make too much of this clean-gene business"? Does Wilma have any other recourse? Or does she just back up and lay down the law again?

Within Wilma's anger is a demand. Once she sees it and recognizes what it means, she can do one of several things:

1. She can *increase* her demand for Bruce to change.

2. Having clearly expressed her feelings (and her demand) she can hold to it or *maintain* it, expecting Bruce to change.

3. She can *negotiate* her need for cleanliness with Bruce's need to find and establish his own values.

4. She can *cancel* her demands and let Bruce work out his room arrangements himself.

Any one of these four possibilities are available to Wilma as a means for her to deal with the conflict. Any one of these four could be the right solution *if it satisfactorily: (1) answers Wilma's personal needs; (2) helps Bruce grow; and (3) improves their relationship.*

Let's look at how this might happen for each of Wilma's possible actions.

1. *Increases demand.* This matches Wilma's need for neatness. It may be the very thing needed to help Bruce examine his values and grow. If so, it improves their relationship.

2. *Maintains demand.* Wilma's needs are upheld. May do the same as No. 1 for Bruce and their relationship.

3. *Negotiates demand.* May help achieve Wilma's needs through Bruce's cooperation, or Wilma may reevaluate her standards.

4. *Cancels demand.* If Wilma can genuinely cancel her demands and live with a messy son, she should do so only if she is persuaded that Bruce can grow with the responsibility of setting his own standards.

Whichever possibility Wilma adopts, she will deliver it to Bruce in an "I message," not the "you message" she has been sending: "You clean up your room or else." The "I messages" might be:

1. *Increases demand.* "I don't know how I can stand to clean your room."

2. *Maintains demand.* "I still feel it is important for me to clean the house the way I think it should be cleaned, but I'm frustrated with your room."

3. *Negotiates demand.* "I want to do something about my feelings about your room, and I'm willing to make a deal that I can live with."

4. *Cancels demand.* "I'm willing to let you look after your own room from now on."

Having made a decision doesn't mean that it cannot be modified and revised as we live with it. The only unchangeables are these basic standards for any choice—(1) that our deci-

32

sion *satisfies our personal needs or demands* (which includes the option of canceling them); (2) that *it helps each person grow;* and (3) that *it improves the relationship.*

Let's summarize the differences between "I messages" and "you messages."

"I messages" reveal feelings without making demands.

"I feel the good work I've been doing isn't noticed."

"You messages" obscure feelings and point fingers of blame.

"You always notice the work Bill does instead of mine."

"I messages" allow the other person to see the effect of his behavior, without exerting pressure.

"I have an idea that if my work was recognized I'd stand a better chance of promotion."

"You messages" demand action while they threaten the relationship.

"If you keep favoring Bill and ignoring my work you'll regret it . . ."

"I messages" encourage the other person to grow and affirm trust in him to handle the situation with responsible behavior.

"Without an honest evaluation of my work, I don't know how to improve what I'm doing and get a promotion."

"You messages" diminish trust and growth. Although such messages 'demand change and improvement, the message implies that growth will not happen without the threat or demand being there.

"You're standing in the way of my promotion and advancement on my job because you won't give my work an honest evaluation."

"I messages" clearly separate the responsibilities in the conflict by defining the personal problems and feelings raised by the other's actions, but without making the other responsible for those feelings.

"I feel as if my work isn't appreciated."

"You messages" confuse responsibilities by leaving little or no room for the other to explain his position. "You messages" prejudge the other person and make him responsible for your feelings.

"You don't care whether I do good work or not."

How simple it would be, if other people could see things our way! Or at least see that our point of view is a legitimate one, instead of arguing about it!

But many times the point of view we defend so vigorously is faulty and should be challenged. Some of us are stubborn about the ideas we cling to—even the wrong ones—and it takes a brave person *who cares enough* to show us the possibilities of a better idea.

Reprinted by permission from *When You Don't Agree,* by James G. T. Fairfield, copyright 1977 by Herald Press, Scottdale, PA 15683.

Chapter 5

Love and Grow

by David A. Seamands

Background Scriptures: 1 Corinthians 13:1-13

Let's begin with the idea that the marriage garden is a place where *love* is intended to *grow*. *Love* and *grow* are the two important words. We've seen the need for growth in our lives; now we will take a closer look at love, specifically the different kinds of love. C. S. Lewis said there are four, and a happy marriage is made up of a balance of all four.

First, there is *need love*.

This is the basic hunger to *be* loved, to be needed and wanted, to belong to someone. This kind of love was acknowledged by God in the beginning: "it is not good that the man should be alone" (Genesis 2:18a).

All of us need to be needed. We want to be wanted. In fact, some people's motto is, "It's better to be wanted for murder than not to be wanted at all." And they do some pretty horrendous things to satisfy their "need love."

There has to be *some* "need love" on both sides in marriage—but the love-starved person who reaches out for any arms he or she can find makes an impossible partner, because of this unquenchable thirst.

You can't be happily married to someone else until you are first happily married to yourself. Otherwise, you will marry out of emptiness and deep insecurity; and "need love" that is too demanding will destroy the very relationship it is trying to establish.

Then there is *eros*—biological, sexual love.

Married love definitely includes its fullest physical expression, and is intended to be filled with joy and ecstasy. When Paul counsels Corinthian couples (1 Corinthians 7:3-5) that marriage partners have rights over each other's bodies and are not to abstain from sexual expression except by mutual consent for an agreed-upon time in order to wholly concentrate on spiritual devotion, after which they are to resume relations, he is plainly implying that eros love is for purposes other than procreation. Eros love is part of the divine design. It is the physical, sacramental expression of the one-flesh relationship.

Third comes *philia* love—comradeship, companionship, friendship.

This, too, was acknowledged in God's providing Adam a helpmate, a partner to share with. How much more fun it would have been to have someone with whom to talk over the names he had picked for all the animals! Sharing, day in and day out, is absolutely essential in any marriage and grows even more so as the marriage matures.

Finally, there is *agape,* the love that comes directly from God himself.

This is the divine love that enables a human to accept another human exactly as he is, the love that can forget as well as forgive, the love that knows no limits or end, the highest form of love.

God created "need love." He created "eros love." He created "philia love." But He did not create "agape love," for He is himself agape love. Therefore, "agape love" is not indigenous; it is not natural to the created order of things. It has to come from outside the order. It is not something that can be developed by human effort.

"I'll love her if it *kills* me!" an irate husband exclaims.

"It's likely to kill both of you in the process!" is my reply.

"Agape love" is a gift. It is God-given, supernatural, redemptive, healing, unconditional love. It is covenant love, commitment love, surrender love—love that is based on the will and does not depend on the emotions. Agape love comes only from God.

There is a balance of these four loves growing together in the garden of marriage. But there are also weeds—some terrible, virulent species which can stunt or stifle or completely stop the growth of love. Then the garden becomes a veritable jungle—a mass of feelings and attitudes and actions that can take over and utterly ruin it.

Let me share from pastoral experience a few of the most common, home-grown, garden variety weeds.

The first is the deadly *turned-head weed.*

This one grows in one direction, but the head faces in the opposite direction. You might call it the "if only" weed. It makes a peculiar noise when the wind blows through it. It whines, "Look what I've given up to marry you." Or, "If only I had married Freddie when he asked me." This weed lives on the memories of bygone days, of former loves, of past opportunities. It lives in a fantasy world of the past which it keeps reinforcing with old memories, old snapshots that should have been burned a long time ago. A letter in the basement which you only look at once in a while . . .

Scores of movies and dramas have been written about this weed: about the husband or wife who hangs onto an old fantasy of the past, an old boyfriend, a might-have-been person. Such a person goes through life systematically destroying his present marriage, his partner, and his children until all is in shambles.

Often toward the end the clever novelist or dramatist brings you to the horrible moment of disillusionment, when our fantasist actually meets the real it-might-have-been person she has dreamed about all these years—only to discover that he is no longer tall, dark, and handsome but fat, bald, and ugly—and obnoxious, to boot.

The shock is all the more magnified by the years of unreal fantasy. The truth is he never *was* quite all that tall or dark or handsome. Thus, life imitates art, only the sad thing is, in life the moment of truth often comes too late and sometimes never comes at all.

A woman who had been married 17 years came to see me. Her marriage was almost on the rocks, and after a few conversations I could see what her problem was. One day, in one of those beautiful moments when the Holy Spirit does what you can't do, she saw it. With a stunned expression on her face, she said to me, "I can't believe it. For 17 years I've been living out of a suitcase."

"What do you mean?"

"You know," she said, shaking her head slowly, "I've never unpacked my bags, I've never settled down, committed myself to my husband and family. All these years I've been doing slow motion video replays of things in the past. It's all been a mirage, and I've been living in it."

Have you?

By commitment, the Bible means that you say yes to one, and no to everyone else. Mentally unpack your bag and make the commitment; this is the way you get rid of this patch of weeds in your garden.

But it takes drastic action. Don't just cut off the top of the "turned-head weed," or it will grow back again, bigger than ever. You've got to get down to the roots, to dig up and throw away some things. There are some doors in your life that need to be slammed and locked and bolted, some things that need to be destroyed and burned and put away.

Then begin thanking God for your marriage partner. (When did you last thank Him for him or her? Has it been a long time? Too long?)

Thank God for what you've gained, not lost. You've gained an opportunity to share your joys and sorrows with another person. You have someone to love you and to belong to, to stand by you in sickness and in health. Someone *real*, not a fantasy image on your secret late show. Every day thank God for the one He has given you. And that noxious "turned-head weed" will wither and die.

Next, we come to the *I-me weed*.

This hardy specimen grows to enormous heights, till you can't see anything else in the garden. Its name comes from two ancient English words, *I* and *me,* that derive from the same root: *mine,* one of the earliest words a child learns.

This weed is a real love-choker! It throttles marriages, turns homes into thickets of in-fighting and competition. The exact opposite of selfless "agape love," this weed quickly makes itself the center of the marriage garden.

"*I* am the most important person! What do *I* get out of it? No, *I* don't care what you've planned; *I* don't want to go there . . ." Some of the favorite expressions of the "I-me weed" are: "My money, my house, my kids, my car, my folks, and my plans." Unless great care is exercised—and this weed is exorcised—you may wind up with "my divorce."

The best way to get rid of the "I-me weed" is to sow the seed of the *our-we* plant. Talk, dream, plan for *our* and *we.* This helps us to think in terms of *our* money, *our* house, *our* car, *our* folks, and *our* plans. And it is so basic, for, as the Bible says, the two *shall* become one. Two *I*'s are now turned into one *we;* two *mines* are turned into one *ours.*

Let's for a moment call an earth-moving implement a spade: the "I-me weed" is a fancy name for plain selfishness. Is it choking the good plants in your garden to death?

Then there's the *clam-up* weed.

This is an insidious pest—not one of the lushest, but one of the toughest to get to the root of. Because when one party "clams up," he makes it almost impossible for the other to find out why.

"What's wrong, Honey?"

Silence.

"Is it something I said?"

The silence of the clam is like unto the silence of the tomb.

"Is it something I didn't say?"

A sigh. Perhaps a little groan. More silence.

This is the dirtiest kind of fighting, because there's no recourse. When this deadly weed takes over, a hush falls over the marriage garden. Silence settles in as repression of deep feelings takes place. Sometimes years go by; things get pushed down and held down. And then one day, the volcano erupts. Suddenly there is a separation and everyone is shocked.

In 1972, the divorce statistics for our country showed an interesting change. If you were to make a chart of the years from 1 to 25 in marriage, the peaks for divorce are the 3rd and 4th years. Then it levels off, until suddenly in the 17th, 18th, and 19th years there comes another sharp rise as veteran married couples break up. The statistics are borne out: we can see it happening among Christians in our churches, everywhere. Why this great tragedy? Mainly because the "clam-up weed" has had all those years to entrench itself, till finally there's a cataclysmic explosion and the marriage garden is destroyed.

The last weed we'll look at is the *wandering affection weed.*

It's small and ugly and its leaves are very sharp. So are its roots: they cut the roots of love under the surface, out of sight, so that love doesn't even know what's happening. Under certain conditions it can be the fastest-growing weed in the garden.

Some of us let this weed get started because we hold onto the myth that when you get married you'll never be attracted to another person again. Ridiculous! Just because you love a person, deeply love him or her, doesn't mean that you lose your power to be attracted to someone else. The circumstances of our society actually encourage this, what with men and women working together in different places. The loosely-knit home life weakens the bond between many couples.

In my office, I have seen people shocked to realize that they are gripped by a strong attraction for "someone else." They never thought it was possible that Christians could have this happen to them. They are plagued with deep guilt.

True marital love has its basis in the will, not the emotions. The fact that you get married doesn't make you automatically immune to temptation. It doesn't change your basic humanity, your masculinity or femininity. It does mean you have made a fundamental choice, a commitment of the will to belong to another "till death do us part."

How do you get rid of the "wandering affection weed"? First, try to nip it in the bud. That's so important! Don't let the little devil get started, because it grows so quickly! In almost no time at all, the wandering glance can become the lustful look. The open sharing and companionship can soon become something deeper. We married Christians really need the antiseptic power of the Holy Spirit surrounding us, to cleanse and purify us in our relationships, the casual ones as well as the more serious.

I've heard it with such sadness—"It began when we were praying together. We became close friends. Suddenly, before we knew it, we were in each others' arms . . ."

Nip it in the bud! That's number one.

But what if you are already in the grip of this dilemma? You feel dry and empty and utterly feelingless toward your married partner. What should you do?

Make a list of everything your wife or husband really likes. Actually sit down and write out a list. Then go out and *do* these things for your husband or wife!

Keep in mind that 1 Corinthians 13—that great description of agape love—says not a word about feelings. It doesn't say anything about them, because *real love is a way of behaving.*

So go and *do* the loving thing for your partner, and keep on doing it. Ask the Lord to change your feelings. Don't worry, if you're obedient, they'll soon fall into line.

William James was a psychologist years ahead of his time. He said, "If you go through the proper motions, the desired emotions are bound to follow." E. Stanley Jones put it another way, equally good. At times, he said, we have to "act ourselves into a new way of feeling, in order to feel ourselves into a new way of acting."

So *do* the loving thing. I give this prescription, and the confused husband goes out the door. In two or three weeks (it never takes longer than that) he's back. He says, "Doc, we're on a second honeymoon!"

42

What happened? "Agape love" came in and refilled the cup of marriage. Natural love was dry and needed to be replenished by His supernatural love.

Is your cup dry? Is the wine of joy, romance, and happiness in your marriage running low? Don't look for another cup; remember the wedding feast in Cana, and take your empty cup to Jesus.

"Fill it with water," He said. Sometimes that means tears of repentance, the "I'm sorry, Honey," the fresh sharing together. It takes a few tears. But He will soon turn the water into the wine of joy and love.

From *Problem Solving in the Christian Family*, by David A. Seamands. Copyright 1975 by Creation House, Carol Stream, Ill. Used with permission.

Chapter 6

Finances in Marriage

by R. E. Zollinhofer

Background Scriptures: Proverbs 22:1-3, 26-27;
23:4-5; Ecclesiastes 5:10

> *A good name is more desirable than great riches;*
>   *to be esteemed is better than silver or gold.*
> *Rich and poor have this in common:*
>   *The Lord is the Maker of them all.*
> *A prudent man sees danger and takes refuge,*
>   *but the simple keep going and suffer for it.*
>   (Proverbs 22:1-3, NIV)
>
> *Do not be a man who strikes hands in pledge*
>   *or puts up security for debts;*
> *if you lack the means to pay,*
>   *your very bed will be snatched from under you.*
>   (Proverbs 22:26-27, NIV)
>
> *Do not wear yourself out to get rich;*
>   *have the wisdom to show restraint.*
> *Cast but a glance at riches, and they are gone,*
>   *for they will surely sprout wings*
>   *and fly off to the sky like an eagle.*
>   (Proverbs 23:4-5, NIV)
>
> *Whoever loves money never has money enough;*
>   *whoever loves wealth is never satisfied*
>   *with his income. This too is meaningless.*
>   (Ecclesiastes 5:10, NIV)

Money may lead to poverty; not only spiritual poverty, but real physical and economical poverty. Money is a major cause of misery, meanness, and marital miscarriage.

There are dangers when there is not enough money, and hardships may result. There are, also, problems when there is more money than is needed. Bad spending habits and lack of respect for money may develop. A person may spoil himself and his mate and may not be equipped to deal with financial reversal. Major debt is a heavy burden for any family to bear, especially when that debt resulted from reckless spending.

The most damaging of these three occurs when a couple is unable to repay their loans, or when repayment demands too large a portion of their income.

It has been said that the family that prays together stays together. However, it is just as true that the family that handles its finances correctly will likely stay together. Carefully managed, money can be the source of great joy in the home. Many

45

of life's pleasant experiences can be known only as they are purchased. Money buys labor-saving devices, fashionable clothes, and comfortable homes. It is no sin to have money to spend, and it certainly makes life easier.

On the other hand, it can be readily demonstrated that neither riches nor poverty are a guarantee of marital bliss. Yet, more marriages come apart because of a lack of money than too much. Let's face it, it's tough to be poor. It is even more agonizing when the anxiety caused by insufficient funds is the result of frivolous spending.

A young couple, with two children, were both employed with better-than-average incomes. They spent all they earned, obtained a home, fine furniture, and a boat. At the time of purchase everything was within their means. Then, the husband lost his job when the company went bankrupt. He was out of work for three months. He found other work, but at a smaller salary. A year later the same thing happened to the wife. She found new employment within four months and at the same salary. By then, they were in arrears with all creditors. Discouraged, they dropped out of church because of embarrassment. They also avoided their family. Fortunately, they never argued or blamed each other, thus divorce was never a threat. Other couples have not been so fortunate.

After many months and consultation with parents and friends, adjustments were made and they began the long, slow road back to financial stability again. But, it took a considerable amount of help and self-discipline.

That story, with variations, typifies many confused and frustrated couples who are on the verge of divorce. Some of those couples have no family to help and no friends to turn to, or else they are too proud to ask for help or advice. Therefore, they increase their misery as monthly bills pile up.

Another family, feeling the money crunch, began to miss monthly payments. Soon the phone began to ring and creditors hounded them. They had their phone number changed and requested that it be unlisted. The creditors then reviewed the credit application and obtained the employer's number. Next, the phone at the place of employment began to ring. A superior of the financially embarrassed man learned what was happening. The man was fired. Can you imagine the hurt, fear, and shame that came down on that man and his wife?

The stories go on and on. The trouble starts just about the same in every case and the damage is often the same. These stories do not have to be. There is a way of writing a better history for each family.

Here are a few guidelines:
1. Counseling before marriage
2. Budgeting
3. Saving
4. Waiting
5. C.O.D.
6. Planning

1. Counseling before marriage

If love is blind, marriage is an eye opener, and money may be a crippler. Few things in life have as great an impact on the marriage relationship as money problems do. It is almost as if marriage ceremonies include the statement, "till debt do us part."

Every couple would do well to consult with their pastor, families, or a family planning consultant about money before marriage. It is not true that two can live as cheaply as one. Some hidden dangers in marriage are: an unawareness of the spending habits of the intended mate, thoughtlessness, inexperience, immaturity, selfishness, and greed. Love may blind many to these faults, but a good pastor or counselor could detect some of these and give advice and help.

2. Budgeting

A most important thing to consider in the family is budgeting. Many couples shy away because it causes friction to talk about it. Others are just unaware of its necessity. However, it is a very rewarding experience to work up a budget and then live with it.

First, list all income. Be sure it is income you can depend on. Do not trust speculation on occasional income that might readily disappear. Next, list all expenditures. Those expenditures should begin with God's tithe, then the essentials: shelter, food, clothing, transportation, insurance, and hospitalization. Prepare a balance sheet. It might look something like this:

Income

His Salary (Monthly)	$1,000 Gross
Her Salary (Monthly)	600 Gross
Total Take-home Pay for Both (Less Taxes)	$1,350 (Approximately)

Expenses

Tithe	$ 160
Housing (Rent)	250
Utilities	125
Food (Including Lunches)	200
Clothing	50
Car Payment	155
Gasoline	50
Insurance	25
Savings	50
Entertainment	50
Furniture	50
Second Car Payment	125
Total Expenditures	$1,290

This would leave $60.00 for all other contingencies.

In the event only one person has an income, the budget would have to allow for spending money for the person staying home.

One thing more, when dealing with the budget, the most capable person in the family should act as money manager, not to rule over the funds but to manage carefully all things pertaining to money. Of course, there must be mutual consent in the whole matter.

A word of caution here. Do not obligate all of your income. There are unexpected repairs, dentists, doctor, replacements that come up every month. There must be money available to meet these needs as they arise.

While these figures may be unrealistic for you, they represent a budget. Each couple must figure their own, but it is essential that both husband and wife see it on paper. Just this simple principle could save trouble down the road.

3. Saving

Many couples defer the establishment of a saving program until some unspecified time when they "can afford it." However, a strategy for meeting emergencies should be a high priority item in financial planning.

The first step in planning for the future is an adequate insurance program. Each couple will need to decide for themselves, with adequate financial counseling, how much insurance they will need if one of them should die unexpectedly. One banker writes, "Life insurance should be considered for protection as it is not basically an investment. For some, however, it is the only investment program they ever have."

Insurance provides two things. It protects you against a financial burden when death occurs, and it is also a type of savings. After a few years the policy develops what is called "cash value." In times of financial distress, the policyholder can borrow at a lower interest rate than a regular loan. To maintain maximum protection, this should be repaid as quickly as possible.

Cash value, however, builds up rather slowly, and rarely provides a suitable savings plan. After the couples' insurance needs have been met, a savings account should be given special attention. This should be a passbook account in a bank, savings and loan, credit union, or similar financial institution. This kind of account allows immediate access to the money in case of emergency. A convenient "rule of thumb" is that a couple should have one-tenth of their annual income in a regular savings account before considering other investments.

4. Waiting

Another wise move on the part of a family is to wait. Not everything has to come in the first few years. Give life time to establish itself. Seniority, salary increases, and savings all take time. It will pay any family to wait before going into debt. There is no need to apologize for not having all the things that others have. Time will permit you to have more at less cost if you wait until you can pay cash. Interest is high on time purchases, and it is wasted money. It buys nothing.

5. C.O.D.

Cash on Delivery is sound fiscal policy. A good shopper can bargain better if he has cash. In most cases, he gets better service. The idea advanced by finance companies—that if you still owe for a product you can get a better guarantee on service for that product—is just not true. The banks and credit card people will not help you if your product is inferior or broken. When buying, purchase from a reputable dealer and question the warranty and return policy of the store. But if you can do it, *pay cash.* It is the cheapest way.

6. Planning

Spend a worthwhile evening planning 10 to 20 years down the road. Take into account your expected income, children, schooling, housing, and retirement. Make your long-range plan, then cut back to the half-way mark. What do you want to do in that period of time? Plan in segments of time—20 years, 10 years, 5 years. This year your plan may change, deadlines may be adjusted, but you will accomplish more if you plan ahead . . . and it is lots of fun. Dream together, even if your dreams cannot come true, it is a loving experience. When you plan, often the impossible dream does become reality.

Some Cautions

1. *Avoid the credit trap.* There is real danger here. Interest is costly, but even more devastating to family happiness, the tendency is to overspend. It is hard to not use a card if you have one available. The urge to buy often overwhelms a person and they use the plastic card. It seems so easy, but it is costly and sometimes disastrous.

2. *Avoid concealment.* Do not hide anything from your mate. Do not make purchases without your mate's knowledge. Do not cover up debt, loss, or anything else.

   This quote from Jonathan Edwards is worth posting in your home. "To keep clear of concealment, to keep clear of the need of concealment, do nothing which you might not do out on the Boston Common at noon day. I cannot say how more and more that seems to me to be the glory of a young man's life. It is an awful hour when the first necessity of hiding anything comes. The whole life is different after that. When there are questions to be feared and eyes to be avoided and subjects which must not be touched, then the Bloom of life is gone. Put off that day as long as possible. Put it off forever if you can."

3. *Watch for selfishness.* It is very easy to want your own needs met first. Be careful of stinginess. Too much frugality is as damaging as not having enough money to make ends meet.

4. *Do not try to buy your wife's (or husband's) love and admiration.* If you need to supply all your mate's wants to keep him happy, your marriage is not based on proper principles. Your mate usually wants only your love, attention, affection, respect, a fair amount of time, and a fair share of material things. Give him, or her, those but avoid buying your mate's love.

One further word. Remember, you are a steward of all that God allows you to earn or have. His tithe is a necessary part of your trustworthiness. Be a good steward and God will honor you with more of His possessions.

Chapter 7

Sometimes
Married Means Lonely

by Robin Worthington

Background Scriptures: 1 Corinthians 7:10-16
2 Corinthians 4:7-18

Even the crackling fire in our family room didn't dispel the slight chill each of us in our group felt as we remembered and shared the times in our married lives we had felt lonely. "The loneliest time of our marriage was right after we moved here from the East," Barbara said softly, twisting her wedding ring as she spoke. "Tom had a job, an identity—and I had nothing."

Tom, sitting beside her on the brick hearth, reached for her hand. "Honey, I was lonely, too, but I kept it to myself because I thought you were having a hard time. Maybe I shouldn't have kept quiet."

"Sometimes a man gets lonely *because* of his job," Paul, a middle-aged businessman, offered. "It's hard to be personal friends with men you're competing against, so you don't talk about your feelings at work. Then your family doesn't understand what goes on at work, so you're left out in the cold both places. That's what *I* call lonely."

"I get caught off balance by the kind of loneliness that just sweeps in like a cold wind from nowhere," I said. "Right before our second child was born, for instance. Suddenly I realized that though it took two of us to make the baby we both wanted, I'd be the only one to go through the delivery room doors, and I'd be the one with all the daytime responsibility for two small children. Then, the next day, the feeling disappeared just as mysteriously as it had come."

"Those out-of-the-blue feelings do pass," agreed Eve, her face lit by the glow of the fire. "It's when a couple can't communicate that they're perpetually lonely. It's a kind of ache in their marriage."

As I gathered up coffee cups and napkins after our guests left, I reflected on the conversation of the evening. Clearly, even happily married couples were not immune to loneliness.

Loneliness hits us all, it seems, with a chemistry unique to each marriage and the people in it. Sometimes the cause is external and other times the source is within the marriage itself. If we look at some of the causes, we will be able to deal better with our own unique pain signals.

Certainly American mobility contributes to our loneliness.

Our culture puts heavy emphasis on popularity, as if our worth were measured by the number of friends we have. Then our corporations and military services move us away from those very friends and confidants. In the highly transient Washington, D.C., area where we once lived, IBM wives joked ruefully that the corporate initials stood for "I've Been Moved."

While these moves may mean advancement up the promotional ladder for the husband, they often bring a sense of isolation to his wife. His business credentials travel with him. Her credentials are seldom transferable. In the new town, no one knows about the Cub Scouts she den-mothered or the successful Halloween ghost house she dreamed up as a hospital fund raiser. She must create an identity all over again, starting at zero. As Barbara had told her discussion group: "When we moved, I wrote back home, 'I hope I don't die here. No one would come to my funeral.'"

Her feelings at the time of the move were typical of many women. She had always had caring people around her. "Parents, brothers and sisters, longtime friends. They were like a mirror telling me who I was. The quiet one. The musical one. The one who did such nice needlepoint.

"Then we moved and I didn't know anyone. I felt I *was* no one, without that reflection from others. Tom was wrapped up in his new job, so during that lonely stretch I had to *give myself* encouragement that I was a pretty neat person. It was like giving a flute solo without an audience. I had to have ears for myself—and do all the applauding.

"I don't want to go through a move again soon, but I did learn that sometimes in loneliness you find your own strength."

Sometimes it is the inner events of matrimony that produce loneliness. The other person really is "other." Marriage experts make a convincing case that all of us carry around in our heads the image of an ideal mate. Interestingly enough, the ideal is often the opposite of ourselves.

Look at the marriages around you (and perhaps your own). Neatnicks marry slobs. Early rising larks marry late-show owls. Elk-hunting men marry women who write sensitive poetry and hide it in the pantyhose drawer. Affectionate women marry aloof men and vice versa.

In fact, studies by one researcher show that the overwhelming majority of people in his test sample married their polar opposites, leading him to quip, "People marry people they'd never dream of having for friends."

Yet it's not too surprising, when we think about it, that people often fall in love with those who have their own missing qualities. We all search for completeness, and we're fascinated that the other person can do what we cannot, whether it is to relate easily to children, work a calculator, run a successful meeting, or build a retaining wall.

Then comes the day when the difference that was an attraction in the beginning becomes a problem to be resolved in the present. The woman who is warm and spontaneous with children now seems like a child herself to the husband who wants to pursue a logical intellectual discussion. The woman who thrives on an active social life finds her husband wants to stay home on the weekends and pour concrete. Suddenly differentness means loneliness.

The temptation is strong to launch a heavy artillery campaign to reform the other person. Marriage counselor Ira J. Tanner, author of *Loneliness: The Fear of Loving,* holds out little hope for the success of such efforts. He writes: "Any attempt to mold our mates in an effort to match them to our fantasies is arrogance on our part and an insult to them. It divides, breeds anger, and provokes even greater loneliness."

The first step in solving the difficulties of difference is, it seems to me, a willingness to acknowledge and respect otherness. Separateness is, after all, the beginning of relationship.

People come to terms with otherness in very concrete, practical ways. Recently I spotted Maggie, a former neighbor, at a community college seminar. I asked her where her husband, Mike, was.

"At the hockey game," she replied with a smile that hinted there was special meaning in her reply.

"We finally agreed to stop trying to make each other over," she explained as she sat down on a folding chair. "Mike and

I enjoy different things. I used to sulk and feel lonesome when he wouldn't come to a group meeting with me. He couldn't understand why I wasn't fascinated with football and mud. We finally realized we can love each other without dragging each other to functions one of us hates.

"Sure, I wish he were here, but I'm glad I'm not at the hockey game, watching grown men bash each other with sticks. And he'll be glad he's not at the concert with me next week.

"We still do plenty of things together—beachcombing with the kids, having our friends over to dinner—but being different does not scare us anymore. Now we *negotiate and appreciate.* Funny thing, we're not together quite as much, but we're not as lonely as we were either."

Differentness can add richness and depth to our marriages if we work at understanding the other person and letting him be who he is.

Often enough we don't really know where the other person is. For one man I know, the shock of two divorces in his family jolted him into realizing how little he was in touch with his wife's feelings—or his own.

"You know how it goes," he said. "You think, 'I won't bring this or that subject up because it'll make her mad. Why rock the boat?' Pretty soon all you talk about is kids and bills. You've grown apart. You're lonesome and you don't even know how you got there.

"Those divorces scared Phyllis and me into action. We've started writing notes down during the day." He pulled a small spiral notebook from his shirt pocket. "She writes down things at home; I do it at work. Otherwise you forget.

"For instance, your emotions are different in the morning and at night. I was moody this morning. Why? I write that down and we talk about it when we get home. She does the same. Maybe the notes would seem silly to someone else, but Phyllis and I are closer to each other than we've ever been before."

Many couples have discovered the technique of exchanging written journals of their feelings. Other couples, uncomfortable with structured exchange, write quick notes to themselves of feelings to discuss with their mates. Each couple can find its own best way.

"Unshared feelings make me feel terribly isolated," says one wife, "but my husband would have a fit if I brought out any piece of paper that looked like a list. He associates that with 'Please put weed killer on the back lawn' or 'Pay the dentist.' So my notes are reminders to myself. After all, I can't blame him for not understanding me if I don't ever tell him that I feel good when he's tolerant of my tennis mistakes or that I get upset when he criticizes my clothes in front of my friends."

Similarly, a wife can't understand her husband's job problems if he doesn't share them with her. She may not grasp the intricacies of inventory control, but she is very likely to understand the people-problems he faces at work.

In spite of the hard sell we've had in recent years on "communication" as an all-purpose remedy, talk won't necessarily cure every form of married loneliness, especially if what we're communicating is blame. When the cause of loneliness is situational—a move, a new job, being home with a new baby, or the departure of our last child—then we need support from our mates, but we also must take individual action for ourselves. The wife who flings the accusation at her husband, "I'm lonely!" might well ask herself instead, "What am I doing about it?"

Often, we must take the first step—and sometimes the second, third, and fourth—to cure our own loneliness. In a new town, it may mean telephoning a likely acquaintance we've met at school or church.

To shed our loneliness before it becomes a second skin, we might volunteer to help in the nurse's room at school once a week; search out other couples for a baby-sitting co-op to free us from the house; sign up for a class in home vegetable gardening. Shared interests and increased personal contacts lead to new and gratifying friendships. These, in turn, take the pressure off our spouses to bail us out of our unhappy isolation.

Still another reason that communication is not a cure-all for married loneliness is a fact often overlooked by the "sharing-is-everything" advocates: Some people talk more than others. Always have, always will. Extroverts and introverts, God created them both, and—like other opposites—they often marry one another.

"Many people never realize how difficult it is for their marriage partners to reveal their inmost feelings and hidden needs," points out one minister and marriage counselor. "Often one mate may be gregarious, impulsive; the other reticent and inhibited. It is costly for the latter to be honest, and his spouse may not sense this fully." In this kind of relationship, the more extroverted partner must move sensitively or his mate will retreat instantly, intensifying the loneliness between them.

There is some married loneliness that only faith can overcome. God may be the only one to whom you can talk about your loneliness at this moment. Unlike some human listeners, He won't interrupt or tell you not to feel what you honestly feel. If you're open to His leadings, He will give you both the strength to endure and the courage to reach out again, for He loves you and your marriage partner.

The results of this kind of prayer may be surprising. One woman said, "After I'd prayed about my loneliness long enough and often enough, God showed me that whenever my husband did reveal a little corner of his feelings, I pounced on him. From trying to live in the presence of God, I've learned a lot about the healing power of human presence. To me it means giving the other person openings to express himself, but being willing to wait without probing or pushing."

From *Marriage and Family Living*, June, 1976. Used by permission.

Chapter 8

Spending Time Together

by Jack C. Stepp

*Background Scripture: Genesis 2:23-24;
3:6-13, 17; Philippians 2:2-8*

It was the day of their wedding anniversary and Gene wanted to do something special for his wife of eight years. He asked his operations' supervisor for the afternoon off. Strolling through the door of his home, he surprised Betty with a kiss, a card, and the announcement that he was celebrating their anniversary by coming home so they could spend time together. In a few moments he settled down on the living room couch fingering the newspaper and glancing occasionally toward the screen which told of the lives of other persons unknown to him. Betty happily retreated to the kitchen to make his favorite meal—a pizza with all the trimmings. She was so happy that Gene had taken the afternoon to be with her on "their day," she phoned my wife to share her excitement. The conversation continued as the pizza was properly made and baked. Betty hurried the conversation to an end. Presenting him with her work of love, she found Gene asleep, sprawled on the couch. Disappointed, she placed the pizza on a nearby table and sat by his head deep in thought. There they were, spending time together.

The above event really happened. But even if it had not, it would still be true to life. Tragically, many couples have not discovered the fine art of spending meaningful time together. The adjective *meaningful* is indeed meaningful. There is a profound difference in being geographically together and "togetherness." A couple may be together in one location for a great deal of time yet not have invaded the inner life of each other's world. Nearness may, or may not, make for intimacy and "togetherness." Persons may be at home together yet living separately.

One lady, so distraught by the absence of a fulfilling and supportive relationship with her husband, went to a counselor for guidance. In the midst of their conversation, she said something every married person ought to understand. She said, "If I'm going to be lonely, I might as well be lonely alone." It is ironic to be in a relationship that promises love, friendship, companionship, mutual support, and confidence only to be disillusioned by loneliness within that relationship. It is possible to live in solitary confinement together. It is devastating to wake up in a marriage only to find that you are living outside your mate's life psychically or spiritually. A couple may eat at the same table and share the same bed and yet seldom touch the inside of each other's world. No marriage will seriously approach the promised life of the wedding vows without spending meaningful time together.

If togetherness is to be worthwhile at all, it must be spent with a sense of purpose involved in it. Spend time together on purpose. Haphazard blitzes may whet the appetite but do little to meet the deeper needs of the marriage partner.

Live in the other's world. Share the pleasant experiences of life together. Know the healing, restoration, and reward that openness and devotion bring. If time together is to be meaningful, it must be on purpose—a mindful expectation and remembrance of the other person of your life's choosing.

Simply, there is a great deal of difference between the quantity and quality in regards to "togetherness." In the illustration that introduced this chapter, what difference was there to Betty whether Gene was sleeping on the couch, or working in the shop as far as her emotional needs and their continuing relationship was concerned? The answer is clear: The amount of time was given greater importance than the quality of their interaction. Both are important to the marriage relationship. It is easy, but disillusioning, to confuse quality with quantity, and vice versa. How can anything of value be fostered without time being given to it in the first place? Marriage is not a finished project at the church altar. It is the doorway of a journey in which time spent together is a promise and ingredient for happiness.

I know the guilt of having discovered that I had placed myself outside my wife's world of mothering and housework, secluded like a monk in my own thoughts and feelings. How she longed to see a slice of me, to spend some moments in the adult world with the one she loved more than any other save Christ. How little I sometimes realize I need her and those tender moments of discovery, actualization, disclosure, and vulnerability. This is the fine art of living together.

How often have I walked through the door of my home discouraged or broken only to return to my work the next day with resolution and vigor because Kay has been the bringer of God's grace and strength in my life. Such cannot happen unless meaningful, quality time is spent together.

On the other hand, did you notice that Betty failed to capitalize on one of her husband's more receptive moments when she bounded off to fix a pizza? What a golden opportunity she missed! Sensitivity to your spouse's receptive or open moments and sharing deeply can have great rewards. Times like these will pave the way for deeper openness.

As always, great fun and friendship takes time to develop. If a couple does not like each other, they have real problems. How happy is the couple who are truly friends, who have fun together, who buy into each other's emotional system, and are willing to expose their own.

Here are a few questions that will help you sharpen your skills in this area.

1. Do you make a point of spending a few minutes each day with your spouse, sharing the day?

2. Does your marriage partner know what you actually do on the job?

3. Do you tend to allow frustrations to accumulate in silence on one hand or be acted out in unjust rage on the other?

4. Would you occasionally break an appointment or schedule time away from your work just to be with him or her?

5. Can you consciously use words to clothe your feelings, aspirations, and thoughts?

6. What things can you do together that would allow a forum for your relationship to deepen?

The Jansens follow a well-worn ritual. Sue is home from work at three. The kids follow anytime from 3:30 to 4:30 and Jim comes in at 5:00 on the dot. At 4 p.m. the TV goes on and Sue begins supper at 5 p.m., amid the varied and hurried schedules of the early evening hours. The family is divided into a number of pursuits and hassles until the favorite TV programs come on. Then, as if mesmerized by the activity of other people's lives, the little congregation settles in for the tenure. However, later one evening, the format went awry—the television set convulsed and went blank. In an effort to revive the picture, Jim hit the side and rattled the set in vain. After taking the back off and looking over the array of wires and tubes he sighed and sat down on the carpet. The children complained. Sue got up to finish her work. After all, what do you do when the TV burns out?

Perhaps the answer is found in recreation that is truly recreating. Recreation can recreate life in your marriage as well as your body, mind, and spirit. Some couples have not learned that the Christian life is to be enjoyed. Instead, they suffer through it. Stress, tension, and guilt feelings can accumulate without a viable outlet. All the while God promises abundant life and pleasures forevermore.

One happy discovery I have made is that recreation helps to relieve the tensions and responsibilities I face daily. What better way to experience the best of life than to spend time recreating with the one you love best?

Here are some suggestions to motivate your thinking in some, hopefully, creative directions.

1. Find a place in your church where you can work together in an area of ministry to others—a Sunday School class, a prayer group, or a calling ministry are examples of what you could do together. Devote your time with purpose on purpose to developing a creative ministry. As you move to help others outside yourself and be the channel for God's grace in others' lives, your own life and marriage will grow. Love is something you cannot keep. You must give it away or it will die.

There is a lot of talk these days that pits the marriage or family against the church. It is a cruel thing to do, to make friends into enemies by resenting church involvements or making them the scapegoat. We can imply it is "more spiritual" to refuse involvement in church life because we need to be "at home" with our husbands or wives only to sit there in front of a TV with our feet up munching popcorn evening after evening. Church life can provide the ever-deepening forum for a together ministry, an extension of and prospering of your love.

2. Find a work project or hobby around the home you both enjoy. Allow continued "bonding" to take place as you work together. Of course the activity must allow for sharing and the art of listening. How many solutions were wrought and possibilities sought as Kay and I labored over a macrame project, or chair in the midst of refinishing, or a room we have decided to clean together! Perhaps we are missing some other real opportunities when we neglect to work together.

3. Buy an inspirational book or magazine to read. Then share your thoughts and feelings. Couple this with light from God's Word and prayer. Make a prayer chart and share in the victories as you date the answers God brings. Let your pre-sleep minutes be together minutes.

4. Take a day off and spend it with your wife or husband. Think of delightful acts of love with which you can surprise your spouse. Phone your wife during the day just to take a break with her. Put a love note in his lunch or pocket. Keep a good sense of humor and enjoy life. Find ways to spur the romantic element in marriage like flowers, cards, a day away, or a small

gift. But more important, give your spouse yourself, your undivided attention, with your gift.

5. Schedule a regular family night. Have a night that the family can look forward to each week and do some "alive" things together. Pack a picnic supper. Fly kites. Ride bikes. Work on your project or ministry together. Play table games. Attend a sports event. Make a cake together. Go window-shopping. Learn to play racquetball. Go canoeing. Visit museums or historical sites. Take a walk or go jogging. Drive down to the boat dock or airport. Sing around the piano together. Make a dried flower arrangement after a walk in the woods. Work on your family history.

6. Go on a couple's retreat over a weekend. Listen to tapes on marriage relationships and discuss them. Spend time holding hands and talking. Sit together in the car for a change. Do things which say, "I want to spend this time with you." Again, give your spouse your undivided attention. As much as anything else, this communicates love.

7. Put the kids to bed together. Share the reading of a Bible story at bedtime. Play together with the children.

8. Make mealtimes positive times. Wait until after the meal to discuss serious problems. Surprise your spouse with candlelight. Call your wife at noon to tell her you are going to take her out for supper tonight.

9. Make your television-watching more meaningful. Have your minds in gear as to the quality of programming you see and its potential impact upon your spiritual life. Use a TV program as a purposeful discussion-starter. Allow the stories to motivate you to be a better husband or wife, Christian, or parent. Do not overdo the relaxation function of TV so that it becomes an escape mechanism or blind habit. Do not allow the TV to be the prime means of input into your mind and heart.

10. Make a few special days in your marriage such as the anniversary and birthday dates. Sit down with your pastor and renew your vows to each other to highlight some anniversary dates. Write a creative wedding ceremony for your spouse. Write a long love letter and mail it so she'll receive it on your anniversary.

Remember that God gave us all equal time, 24 hours per day, to find meaningful time to spend together with our "beloved." Don't put off until tomorrow what can and should be done today.

Plan purposefully. As has been said, "We don't plan to fail, but we fail to plan." Be participators rather than spectators. And don't wait until the TV burns out! Have fun spending meaningful time together.

Chapter 9

Who's in Charge Here?

by Colleen Townsend Evans and
Louis H. Evans, Jr.

Background Scriptures:
Ephesians 5:15-27; 1 Peter 3:1-7

There is a lot of pain in many marriages—much of it rooted in the problem of authority.

Kirk was a strong individual, highly creative and well known in business circles. His wife, Carolyn, was a gifted person, energetic, efficient, imaginative, and one to throw herself with all her might into anything she did. But she didn't have much opportunity to exercise her strengths. To say that Kirk was difficult to live with would be an understatement. He was bossy, demanding, not always ethical, and often insensitive to other people's feelings—especially to Carolyn's. He took it for granted that she would go along with him without question.

Some years ago Carolyn told me she had to make a decision. She had tried to have an honest, open discussion with her husband, but he couldn't handle it. He interpreted her concern over his behavior as criticism and went into a rage. It was her complete approval and absolute acquiescence he demanded, nothing less. So Carolyn had to decide between ending the marriage by exercising her strengths—or yielding in every way to her husband. She chose to yield.

Carolyn realized she had a limited number of choices. She could go through the war of separation and divorce—and war it would be—leaving emotional, financial, and spiritual devastation in its wake. Or she could submit to Kirk's pathologies, learning to deal with his tirades and self-centeredness, and hoping that some day Kirk might change.

In choosing to submit to her partner she was giving up the ideal of an open, honest, and shared life. Instead she would have to bite her tongue, swallow her pride, and put a lot of her creative abilities into cold storage. But that was the only way she saw of saving their marriage. Carolyn had bought a kind of "peace."

Some forms of peace are not as creative as others. In Carolyn's case it meant the loss of some outstanding human potential; and yet all was not lost. Some of the time Kirk was a delight—alive, interesting, jovial, even thoughtful, and certainly never a bore! There were compensations, and Carolyn chose to live with them. It was her choice, and I won't fault her for that!

Carolyn's decision was not without its costs. Part of the strain she bore was evident in painful migraines. As years went on, her three children—fine people—carried scars that caused serious trouble. That was a big price to pay for "peace."

If Carolyn had chosen the first alternative, that of divorce, she would have refused to submit, and there would have been a rupture in the relationship. Perhaps the cause would have been tagged "immaturity," "an inability to deal with frustration," "a lack of communication skills and ways of dealing with anger," or maybe it would have been described as an escape from a demeaning, destructive partnership. Whatever the label, the experience would have been painful.

The second alternative meant submitting to another's weakness and living with pain—but keeping the marriage together. In making her choice Carolyn followed what she felt was the biblical view of submitting to one's husband in all cir-

cumstances. Hadn't Paul said, "Wives, be subject to your husbands, as to the Lord. For the husband is the head of the wife as Christ is the head of the church, . . . As the church is subject to Christ, so let wives also be subject in everything to their husbands" (Ephesians 5:22-24, RSV*)? Peter said the same thing: "Likewise you wives, be submissive to your husbands, so that some, though they do not obey the word, may be won without a word by the behavior of their wives . . ." (1 Peter 3:1).

The Pharisees of Jesus' day would have agreed with Carolyn. They took God's curse on woman seriously: "To the woman he said, 'I will greatly multiply your pain in childbearing; in pain you shall bring forth children, yet your desire shall be for your husband, and he shall rule over you'" (Genesis 3:16).

In the Jewish culture of the New Testament, a woman was definitely a second-rate citizen. Sons inherited land, but daughters received only maintenance. If a wife found anything, it belonged to her husband, as did the work of her hands. Even a woman's inheritance, should there be no male to receive it, could be used by her husband for his desires. A woman was not given a teaching position among the laity in the synagogue—if she had a question, she could ask her husband when they got home. The cultural conditioning was so deep it is not surprising that it found expression in the teaching of the New Testament writers themselves.

But let us take a second look at the biblical material. It appears there are four phases to humanity in Christ: (1) created innocence; (2) the Fall; (3) recreation in Christ; and (4) glorification. I will not get into the last, except to say that any Christian who is aware of the promise of Christ and believes it, looks forward to that day of Christ's triumphal return. At this point, however, I want only to look at the first three phases.

The first was the state of innocence in which man and woman were created with a kind of parity. God created mankind male and female. "And God blessed *them,* and God said to *them,* 'Be fruitful and multiply, and fill the earth and subdue it' . . ." (Genesis 1:28, italics mine). Evidently the potential for dominion was given to both male and female. When God created woman, He created her as helper (in the Hebrew, *azar*) to man. But this word *azar* does not imply inferiority or second-rate status. God himself is *azar* to man, "A very present help in time of need." If anything, the word indicates man's incompleteness without woman—his need for her, even as man is incomplete without a relationship with God. Likewise, woman needs man. So close is the need factor that when man was presented with woman, he cried out, "Bone of my bone, and flesh of my flesh!" His very joy was an expression of his need for her. In this phase of humanity, male and female became one flesh. The two were one. They shared a unity of need and complementation.

In the second phase of humanity, that of the Fall, all of life came under the curse of sin. The relationship of man and woman was affected in that man became the ruler of woman, and the wife from that time on was subject to the authority of her husband. The earth was subject to the futility of mankind's distorted dominion, and man himself was cursed to wrest his living from a thistle-filled and thorn-bearing earth. We must remember that all the Old Testament was written during this phase of the Fall and the curse. It was during this phase that Pharisaism was born and developed, with all its legal rules and burdens that Christ described as "heavy burdens placed on people's backs which [the Pharisees] would not lift a finger to lighten" (see Matthew 23:4). Christ was angered by the insensitivity and judgmentalism that pointed a finger at outward behavior without attempting to understand the inward need of the individual. It was that burdensome legalism that drew Paul's sharpest criticism—that the law could not give life or liberate souls oppressed by the curse.

Thank God, we are not stuck in the mire of this second phase. In Christ we have moved on to the third phase of humanity. Through His death and victorious resurrection we have been set free from the curse. In Him we are made new creatures! Here, in this third phase, the image of God's original design is replacing the old forms of legalism and subjugation. "The old has passed away and the new is in the process of becoming!" (see 2 Corinthians 5:17). Old inferiorities are eliminated; woman has become again the "helper," the peer of man. ". . . there is neither male nor female; for you are all one in Christ Jesus. And if you are Christ's, then you are Abraham's offspring, heirs according to promise" (Galatians 3:28-29). Former lords have become servants after the example of Christ striving to bring everyone to maturity in Christ (see Colossians 1:28). Husbands now are to give up their lives for their wives as Christ gave up His life for the Church, that they might be presented before Him "in splendor," the splendor of their full maturity. The subjugations once operating under the law are not removed. Man's subjugation to the law, woman's subjugation to man, mankind's subjugation to death, are now replaced by all of mankind's subjugation to Jesus Christ. Every man, woman, and youth has direct access to Jesus Christ through the Holy Spirit. And through the same Spirit, Jesus Christ has access to the mind and will of every man, woman, and youth.

Therefore, if anyone puts any other relationship ahead of that to Jesus Christ, he or she is not worthy of Christ (see Matthew 10:34-39).

Instead of lordships that hold others in inferior positions, those who have experienced Christ's redemption are called to a life of service. Now, as Christians, we submit to one another out of reverence for Christ, out of reverence for His example of servanthood, out of reverence for His liberating death and resurrection, out of reverence for the gifts that His Holy Spirit creates in each believer.

The Christian wife submits herself to her husband—of course! My wife submits to me in a hundred different ways! But that is not all. I also submit to her. The Spirit calls us to a mutual submission. "Be subject to *one another* out of reverence for Christ" (Ephesians 5:21, RSV) is the key verse here (my italics), and *mutual submission* is the overall theme of the verses that follow. A wife is to submit to her husband "as to the Lord" (Ephesians 5:22)—but that does not mean that her husband *is* her lord. She is to serve her husband in the line of serving Christ. (The Greek word meaning "as" indicates intention, the intention of a wife to serve her husband as he attempts to achieve his dominion over some part of God's creation—just as she serves Christ and the realization of His kingdom.)

Compare Ephesians 5:22 with its parallel passage, Colossians 3:18: "Wives, be subject to your husbands, as is fitting [proper] in the Lord." This means to us that wives are to please the Lord primarily—and then they are to submit to their husbands as the husbands labor for the Lord's kingdom. A Christian wife will submit whatever resources she has to undergird her husband in his efforts to complete Christ's ministry. She will go with him where he feels God is leading him to work, because he is probably the chief breadwinner. She submits to the valid demands made upon her because of the scheduling involved in his work; she makes the way straight for his endeavors. She is indeed his "helper," someone he needs for his completion, just as he needs the Lord and His resources.

If, however, the husband demands something that is outside the will of Christ and requires the wife to give up those things that belong to Christ or to others, then his wife is under no obligation to obey her husband if in so doing she must disobey Christ, her Lord. Any husband who makes such demands on his wife simply demonstrates his foolishness and misplaced ego.

Some Christian teachers insist that a woman should go along with *anything* her husband asks because he is her "lord." After listening to some of the things such husbands demand of their wives—whether in scheduling priorities or in sexual activities—I am convinced that a wife only reinforces her husband's arrogance and demeans herself by submitting to him. Nobody wins by such appeasement. The wife who goes along with a husband's desire when she feels it is contrary to Christ denies her Lord and permits her husband to stumble headlong into a pit of error.

When the question comes up, "Who's in charge here?" the Christian wife should be able to say, clearly and boldly, "Jesus Christ."

A few years ago, when I was considering a call to another church, Colleen exercised a strong influence on my decision. She confronted me, mildly but firmly, because she thought I was not open to the new situation. (I wasn't. I had five good reasons why I shouldn't go!) Finally she said, "Honey, I just don't think you're open-minded about the matter!"

At first I smarted under the confrontation, but she jarred me loose from a "dead center" position. We agreed that I should go away for a few days and pray the thing through. On my return I was "in neutral gear," willing to go or willing to stay. In this attitude we went to the new city, preaching in a nearby church, and met with the committee for a long afternoon of openness and candor that I doubt would have been possible if I had either desperately wanted the position or had been close-minded about it. We put all our cards on the table, as honestly as we could. When the call came, *I* accepted it. It was *my* decision. And yet *we* accepted it. It was my decision and I knew Colleen would go along with whatever I decided, once I gave open consideration to it. But we talked and prayed it over so thoroughly that our minds had a common response when the voice on the other end of the phone said, "It is the unanimous decision of the committee . . ." and so on, and so on. I felt good about letting my wife influence my life. Her sensitivity, her gift of discernment, were much-needed elements. If I had been hard-headed about it, I could have denied her challenge and missed God's direction. In that case, there would have been grave doubts about the equality of my leadership. Jesus Christ is her Lord, not I, and when she submits to His Lordship, I am blessed.

Yes, husbands also submit to their wives, loving them "as Christ loved the church and gave himself up for her, that he might sanctify her . . ." (Ephesians 5:25-26). To me this passage means that Christ loves the Church, that He wants her to be all that she can be, and that He gives himself to the Church, to bring her to her full potential as God designed her, in the splendor of her maturity, cleansed of anything that would hold her back from the full realization of God's design. In doing this Christ is definitely in charge; there was no doubt about His Lordship. But His style of Lordship turns authority right side up for the first time in history. He becomes a Servant-Lord. I believe this to be the model for the Christian husband.

Excerpted from *My Lover, My Friend,* by Colleen Townsend Evans and Louis H. Evans, Jr. Copyright © 1976 by Fleming H. Revell Company. Used by permission.

*All scripture quotations in this chapter are from the *Revised Standard Version of the Bible* (RSV), copyrighted 1946, 1952, © 1971, 1973, and are used by permission.

Chapter 10

Romance: To Like

by Gordon MacDonald

Background Scriptures: Ephesians 5:28-31

In the Parker and Hart cartoon, "The Wizard of Id," a medieval knight with the innocuous name of Rod always seems to be one step behind the tempo of everyone else. That trait is painfully obvious on one moonlit night when Rod finds himself with a lovely princess who says to him:

"Rod, there's something I've always wanted you to do."

"What's that?" Rod asks.

Breathlessly she responds, "Take me in your arms and . . ."

"Shhh . . . hold it," Rod interrupts, putting his hand over her mouth. "I think I heard my horse whinny."

Rod, you blew it! You are apparently always going to be a loser; no romance for you.

With the possible exception of Rod the dumb knight, there is hardly a person in our culture who is not drawn to the idea of romance. We smile inwardly and perhaps even envy the freshness of a young boy and girl who seem lost to the world as they enjoy one another. We call it romance, surrender it to the young, and allow ourselves to believe that romance tends to decline in force with a maturing marriage. But if we have lost it, we quietly admit that we would like to reclaim it.

It is difficult to define romance; it is more of a series of pictures of a relationship than a hard and fast definition. But it appears to center in the "up-front" part of the experience men and women have together. It is the most visible of all the things they do in relating to one another. I think it may include all of the qualities we actually lump together when we say of a member of the opposite sex, I *like* him, or I *like* her.

As a Christian, I have often been instructed that I should love other people. I've heard little about liking them. That was assumed, I guess. You do not hear much about "like" in marriage either. It almost seems to be an absurd question: Do you like the one to whom you are married? But the answer may not be as obvious as one would first think.

An Episcopal rector was retiring, and those of us who knew him planned a farewell luncheon. In the after-dinner discussions, I asked him to recount for us what he thought might have been his most speechless moment. Instantly he recalled such an occasion when he had first entered the ministry. He had been asked to officiate at the funeral of a woman who had never attended church. When he arrived at the funeral parlor to meet the family, he saw only the dead woman's husband. The funeral director told the young minister that the two had been married for 57 years.

My friend approached the husband at the casket, and the only thing he could think to say was, "Fifty-seven years is a long time." His speechlessness came when the old widower said without hesitation, "Too long; she was meaner than blazes."

Obviously, living with a person does not guarantee that you will like him or her. It is quite possible simply to tolerate another person, having worn each other down to the point where the marriage becomes simply a convenience for both partners. The home is relatively peaceful; life goes on with few storms. What has happened is that two people have become amiable roommates, bound together by habit, by economic convenience, and geographic proximity. But like each other? No! The spark has been gone for years.

I am convinced that wholesome love normally emerges through the relational process of "like." Liking someone is generally an emotional experience. And our emotions are usually the gateway to all of the other relational capacities that we have. This is not always the case. I have dealt with people intellectually whom, at first, I did not like. If the biblical definition of love is to serve, I think there have been times when I loved someone I found it hard at first to like.

But in relationships between men and women, *like* is almost always the starting point. Even as *like* is a prelude to mature love, its death is the preface to the disintegration of love. For when two people stop liking each other, their love will soon begin to die also.

There will be some following my thinking who will resist my fine tuning of difference between love and like. But an artificial separation of the two may in the long run help us understand the different threads of relationship which are being woven into this positive concept of cleaving.

Like is the first of the levels of cleaving. Just as cleaving is a positive and deliberate effort to cross relational barriers, the component parts of cleaving—liking, sharing, and serving —are positive and deliberate. But if you must start anywhere in evaluating these different levels, *like* is the most suitable place. For me *romance* and *like* are the same basic experience.

Discovering Romance

There is a curious fact about the three progressively deeper levels of feeling, sharing, and serving. The mastering of the first level makes it easier to move to the second; the mastery of the first and second make it still easier to move to the third. Thus in talking about romance, we are describing something which will ultimately make it easier to share and serve.

Part of this effort is to make ourselves likable. Have you ever asked yourself if you are likable? I find it easiest to like likable people. That should teach me that it is important for me to be likable so that my partner can like me to the fullest possible extent.

Likability may depend upon a number of different qualities. These may differ from one relationship to another. Listing a number of them can give us some opportunity to evaluate our relationship and determine our level of likability. In the final analysis, each couple will develop its own combination of traits upon which likability is judged.

Likability Based upon Physical Attraction. A woman in her mid-30s has come to visit me at my office, and she shares the story of a personal struggle that she thinks is very unusual. Her husband, she says, cannot keep his eyes off attractive women. She speaks of the personal anguish she goes through whenever they are in a group where there are women who are dressed in ways that accentuate their figures. It makes no difference where they are together: shopping, attending services at church, or a PTA meeting. She can depend on her husband to pick out the most striking women in the vicinity and stare at them at every opportunity.

She emphasizes that their marriage is a good one, that she does not feel that it lacks affection, and that they are both committed Christians. What is the problem? Why does her husband's behavior make her feel so inadequate? Is it a sign that he is dissatisfied with her?

My first task is to convince my visitor that her husband's behavior is not that unusual. While it is not necessarily excusable, it is also not uncommon. Most men are quite conscious in any crowd of the more attractive members of the opposite sex.

This woman's husband has fallen for the line the culture has sold him. While he has been created to appreciate honest beauty, he has gone beyond that and achieved a taste for an oversensualized attractiveness. The two of them are going to have to confront the problem together, and he will have to know how much he is hurting her by his roving eye. In the meantime, I try to point out to the frustrated wife that it is important in her own life to become as physically attractive to her husband as possible. This will make the problem's solution that much easier.

I caution her that I am not suggesting that she enter as a participant in the sexual sweepstakes and compete with other women. But I want her to see that her husband is by instinct and culture an admirer of feminine beauty. The problem he has can be addressed as she helps meet that need by making herself as appealing as possible.

Physical attractiveness is a component part of likability. If we want to be liked, we must think about how to make ourselves as honestly attractive to the one we love as we possibly can. Many Christians rebel against this concept, thinking it to be sensual or carnal. They enter a wicked circle. Certainly an overemphasis upon physical attractiveness can lead to a twisted sensuality, but that can also happen in the lives of men and women who are created to appreciate beauty but find little of it in their spouses. Rather than repudiating this need, the Christian man or woman can master it to the extent that God meant for it to play a part in our lives together.

Likability Based upon Verbal Expressions. Saying how we feel is also important to romance. Partners in romance learn how to put their feelings into words. It is as important for one to say certain things as it is for the other to hear them said. Without words, feelings are never solidified, and we are left to guess how the other one feels.

Romance depends upon the frequent and varied expression of love feelings. It was not long after my own wedding that I began to discover the excitement of creatively expressing myself to Gail, my wife. I learned, for example, that a phone call sometimes during the day that had no special purpose except to express love was a welcome relief for both of us.

Cards sent through the mail offered a surprise, and I learned to make a stop at the card store to pick out a few special verses which might share how I felt.

Elizabeth Barrett Browning had this in mind when she took her pen and shared with her lover her own codewords of verbal romance:

> *How do I love thee? Let me count the ways.*
> *I love thee to the depth and breadth and height*
> *My soul can reach, when feeling out of sight*
> *For the ends of Being and ideal grace.*
> *I love thee to the level of every day's*
> *Most quiet need, by sun and candlelight.*
> *I love thee freely, as men strive for right.*
> *I love thee purely, as they turn from praise.*
> *I love thee with the passion put to use*
> *In my old griefs, and with my childhood's faith.*
> *I love thee with a love I seemed to lose*
> *With my lost saints—I love thee with the breath,*
> *Smiles, tears, of all my life! And, if God choose,*
> *I shall but love thee better after death.*

Likability Based upon Appreciation. Romance needs appreciation. Human beings need to know that they are making an important contribution to someone's life. In counseling I have found this to be an area of major breakdown in relationships. I have visited with a number of wives who openly wept as they shared the frustration of having a husband who never appears to notice what they do to make the home a significant place. Women taken for granted, who are unappreciated, sooner or later have to find another outlet for their creativity and desire to please. A few unfortunately find it in the temptation of another relationship. Most will find it in a preoccupation with church work, community activities, or the PTA. There must be appreciation found somewhere.

There is a brightness about husbands and wives who create opportunities to recognize their spouses' attractiveness, their faithfulness to great and small details.

It may be a valuable exercise to sit down and ask yourself what 10 things your spouse has done in the past week to make your life different and enjoyable. List them, and find three different ways to express appreciation for them.

Likability Through "Crazy Times." That is what we call them anyway. Romance requires them: times when a couple breaks the routine and does those things that bring a laugh or a memory. A crazy time can be a moment when a practical joke is shared, or it can be a memory that is purchased by going out for an evening or a weekend. In our marriage we may not have many material investments; we have chosen to make our investment in memories, and we have piled up a lot of them.

One day Gail got wind of an unexpected check I'd received in the mail from a publisher. It wasn't a large sum (publisher's checks usually aren't), but she thought that if she cashed it for me, she could use five dollars for something very important. When I left the check for her to pick up, I attached the following poem which would help remind her that only five dollars of it was hers.

> *I think that I shall never see*
> *A girl that's lovelier than thee.*
> *A girl whose touch is soft and warm;*
> *A girl whose figure is right in form.*
> *But one thing must be clear, by heck,*
> *She had better not spend this entire check.*

Maybe it wasn't Kilmer, but it was a time for a special laugh and a memory. Crazy times can be spontaneous if you are deliberately looking for them. But many of them have to be planned in advance. If a couple has children, there are occasions to include them, but there are also times when they should be sent in the opposite direction while husband and wife break free to dote on one another. Good romancing takes time and privacy; we cannot afford to let it pass by.

Likability Based upon Touching. Romance not only feeds on physical attractiveness, appreciation, affirmation, and crazy times, but it needs a certain level of physical touching. This is not necessarily sexual contact, but movements which bring a couple into the intimate circle of proximity, a circle no one else is permitted to enter.

We need to be touched, stroked, held, kissed, and rubbed. Among the saddest moments that I face in counseling are those spent with a man or woman who is alone in a marriage—alone in the sense that the spouse has lost all desire for touch. Lionel Whiston recalls the husband who crept up behind his wife at the kitchen sink and kissed her on the back of the neck. She reacted in an irritable fashion and said angrily, "Don't kiss me while I'm in the kitchen." The husband was heard to mutter as he exited in a somewhat deflated fashion, "It will be a long time before I kiss you anywhere."

The holding of hands while walking down the street says many things. To each other it says, "I'm glad to be connected with you." To the world it says, "We belong to each other and we are proud to declare the fact." A wife sitting next to her husband in the car says by her actions, I like to be as close as I can whenever possible. The enjoyment of a morning good-bye kiss not only gets the day off to a right start, it may reaffirm for the children something they constantly need to know: Mom and Dad love one another, and that means everything's all right for us, too.

This is the time to pose the question that actually outlines the entire spectrum of romance: How does my partner wish to be loved? To be tender is to ask that question and then to answer it in actions. Too many of us find it simple to love our spouses the way *we want to love* them. I come home for a free evening and get comfortable in the living room with a book. When I go to bed, I pride myself that I have spent an evening with Gail. But I haven't. I have loved her in a convenient way—the way I wished to love. In so doing, I failed to ask the question, first of myself, and then of her, how does she wish to be loved this evening? Perhaps she would like me to accompany her on a trip to the market. "I like to show the other women that you are mine," she says. Marketing is not my way of loving, but it may be the way she wishes to be loved that night.

A man went into a card store to buy a birthday card for his wife. He finally found a very ornate one which carried this message: "Your love is worth the world and all its treasures." He asked the clerk how much it was. "That one is 95 cents," he was told. The man frowned. "Don't you have something that's a little cheaper?"

Romance is not cheap, but its price comes not in the payment of money. It only costs the giving of oneself in a relationship which says, "I really like you!"

Adapted from *Magnificent Marriage*, by Gordon MacDonald, Tyndale House Publishers, 1976. Used by permission.

Chapter 11

Emotional Needs and Responses

by Larry and Aarlie Hull

Background Scriptures: Genesis 1:24-31;
2:18-25; 1 Corinthians 7:1-5

Editor's Note:

Larry and Aarlie Hull are a married couple living in Centralia, Wash., with their five children. He is an orthopaedic surgeon; she, a housewife and free-lance writer. Each of them has written half of chapter 11. They have been asked to describe, from their perspective, how a husband and a wife would like to be treated, and how they can meet the emotional needs of their spouse. Neither of them wrote in response to what the other had to say. But, obviously, their words come out of the reservoir of respect and love they share together.

Larry writes:

What does a 41-year-old, father of five, orthopaedic surgeon, and churchman, who is tired and behind schedule have in common with my fellow man?

My emotional needs vary from nil to overwhelming—and you thought that fickleness was the prerogative of ladies? So, as I bare my "emotional soul," hopefully you can identify with me. Please hold your letters of counsel as I am already behind in my reading and correspondence.

You don't amount to a hill of beans. As a kid on a farm, that statement seemed to have rather frequent application. Today, as a husband, I still want to be reassured that I have more worth "than a hill of beans." As a husband, how is my worth affirmed? Despite the wrinkles, and increasing transparence of my gray hair, I want to know that in my home I am a man among men.

Aarlie, let me know that I am still a pretty super guy, vigorous, fun, and challenging. Let me know that I'm still attractive to you.

I hope my wife will **recognize all the important things I do.** Most of life is routine; most jobs are routine. What I do may be dull, but it is still important. I enjoy talking about the recent orthopaedic advances, the new office equipment I have acquired, my present half-finished home projects, and, oh, yes, the neat way I mowed and trimmed the lawn.

Aarlie, continue to recognize my small accomplishments and they will probably increase in frequency and significance.

Treat me kindly in the presence of others. Do you remember your most embarrassing moment? More likely than not, it related to being put down or made to look foolish in front of someone else, particularly those near and dear. Laughing at an idea, belittling a job or assignment, or pointing out shortcomings to others may make interesting conversation in public, but contribute to long silent spells at home. The classic statement, "Oh, he is only a _____," or, "He is just one of the flunkies." A husband may be only a flunkie at work, but he needs to be reassured that he is a very important flunkie, at least in the eyes of his spouse.

Aarlie, I have always appreciated the way you have been complimentary of me and to me in the presence of others.

The primary role of husband, and the secondary role of father, provides opportunity for either the greatest sense of worth or the feeling that "you don't amount to a hill of beans."

We feel that the greatest gift we can give to our five growing children is a genuine love between Mom and Dad. Yet, **my emotional needs as a husband are tightly woven together with my success and fulfillment as a father.** Positive reinforcement of desirable fathering traits is more compelling and helpful to me than deriding the obvious shortcomings. Words like, "I sure can't do it without you and your help with the kids," tend to bolster my efforts if not in fact "puff me up" as a father.

It may not be fashionable in this day, but Dad is still considered "the big boss" in our family which not only builds my ego but gets my wife out of some tight on-the-spot jams at times. "We'll talk to Dad about it later." Have you heard that one?

Aarlie, it is fun being Dad to your children, and to receive your vote that sometimes "Daddy knows best."

What we are is obviously more important than how we look, seem, or act. However, **appearance and demeanor are at times critical.** As a husband I must treat my wife as I would like to be treated. Thus those items that I can change and improve should receive my attention.

Neatness and cleanliness better than carelessness and poor hygiene.

Masculinity for males just as important as femininity for females.

Patience is better than impatience.

Diligence and personal discipline more attractive than slothfulness and inconsistency.

Softness and tenderness more desirable than harshness and a callous spirit.

A trim body is more pleasing than excess fat and poor conditioning.

Aarlie, I have always appreciated and enjoyed the attractive, trim, soft, feminine, patient, modest, and disciplined traits that make you, you. I love your appearance and demeanor.

A crummy tennis partner. About once every two years, when the weather is nice, the kids cared for, and there has been an unexpected cancellation of a previous engagement, my wife and I play tennis together. She likes to tap the ball, rest a lot, and stop often to sip a soft drink. I really prefer to work up a sweat, kill the ball, and play with a serious vengeance. So, you can easily see that as tennis players we are not terribly compatible. I am pleased however that this does not carry over into the sexual, academic, and spiritual aspects of our life.

As a husband, one of my emotional needs is **sexual fulfillment.** It has been fun to mature as a husband and realize that the superlatives in our physical relationship are a direct product of the gentle, caring, thoughtful concern of the other areas of our marriage. Sexual fulfillment is then a by-product of a good marriage and not the giant Band-Aid for a not-so-good marriage.

Academic compatibility comes most consistently when one tries to focus on similarities and not passionately held diverse ideas. In the 17 years of our marriage, many of the striking differences have come and gone. With open discussion, persuasion, insight, and becoming as one, we have fewer strongly held differences—a few bastions notwithstanding. I am learning that qualifying phrases such as "it seems to me," or "another way to look at it is," or "could it be that," have solved a lot of unnecessary verbal conflicts.

Sexual and academic compatibility have been meaningful to our marriage, but the most exciting phase of our marriage is that of spiritual compatibility. This is the most intimate level of compatibility. **Spiritual compatibility** includes open discussions of spiritual concerns, being able to pray together, and to share common spiritual goals.

It may seem elementary, but singing together, praying together, attending church together, team teaching a Sunday School class or Bible study, attending couples' retreats, and having a united outreach project helps build exciting spiritual compatibility. We first started praying together at night after the light was out. Obviously a dim, but nevertheless important start.

As a husband I do not always relish the responsibility but feel it is important to be reminded that spiritual leadership is the responsibility of the husband.

Aarlie, pray and encourage me to press on to greater spiritual depths so I may provide meaningful leadership to you, L. D., Heather, Amy, Bethany, and Dean.

Visiting your mother again? Cutting the umbilical cord does not always follow tying the knot. Leaving and cleaving are often articulated phrases that need to be practiced. It, no doubt, is healthy in some new marriages to be away from family and in-laws to assist in the process of developing reliance on one another. In just such a setting, I quickly learned the great value of family and in-laws.

However, whether Mom-in-law or Mom is across the backyard or across the ocean, a husband needs to know that his wife desires his presence, counsel, and assistance even more than that of her mother. Being placed second on the list of consultants to one's mother-in-law, or anyone else, is a rejected feeling. When visiting either family, being attentive to each other and assisting in the care of the children makes the visit more pleasant for all.

The birth of a child can bring unusual stress to the husband-wife relationship. Children do not cement an otherwise fragile marriage. Thus, it is important to create a strong marriage before procreation of children. As soon as possible following the birth of the child, redetermine priorities of relationships. Time alone together without the children is necessary for me as a husband and doubly important for my wife.

Aarlie, can you remember the quiet evenings alone with candlelight, soft music, and lazy walks? I can hardly remember them. Please forgive me for not creating more times for lazy walks, gentle breezes, and if still available, soft music.

Willing to go along for the ride. In the good old days it was "How would you like to go along for the ride?" Of course, the ride had no true purpose except to be with the one you loved.

Times are changing and ride is a very serious trip with eternal consequences to both of us and our progeny.

Shared goals and dreams represent one of the more beautiful facets of marriage. Kindred spirits, hands clasped, mutual resolve can make the worst task a breathlessly scintillating experience. This year we are sharing our goals openly so they become true shared goals and dreams. The devil's most visible adversary is a strong, Christ-centered home where husband, wife, and children share mutual spiritual goals and become more than conquerors through Christ.

Aarlie, thank you for fulfilling my life in a thousand different ways and for "going along for the ride" of a lifetime.

Aarlie has this to say:

Larry and I were married one lovely June day. Today, five children and 17 years later we have known many of the circumstances and emotions offered by life. Our circumstances have ranged from near poverty to affluence, from childlessness to a house full of kids, from a small, one-room apartment to a large home with space to spare. We have been carefree and worried, fulfilled and frustrated, rested and tired, encouraged and depressed, happy and sad. Our circle of friends include every spectrum of the socioeconomic ladder. We have observed, and experienced firsthand, that real happiness is found in good relationships with God and our fellow man. As M. R. DeHann writes, "The nearest thing to heaven on this earth is a Christian family and the home where husband and wife, and parents and children, live in love and peace together for the Lord and for each other. The nearest thing to hell on earth is an ungodly home, broken by sin and iniquity, where parents bicker, quarrel, and separate, and children are abandoned to the devil and all the forces of wickedness."

The basic instruction the Bible has for husbands is that they love their wives as Christ loved the Church and gave himself for it (Ephesians 5:25). I don't mind saying that to love anyone as Christ loved the Church is a mind-boggling thought. Further, for a husband to love his wife as Christ loved the Church

91

means he must put her life and happiness above his own. To that kind of love, one young wife exclaimed, "It'd be easy for me to submit to my husband if he loved me like that!" It not only would be easy, it would be almost impossible for a woman with normal instincts not to submit to a man exhibiting that kind of love.

This sounds all well and good, but how is it accomplished? How do you actually muster up whatever it takes to love like that? It is not easy and that is why so many marriages do not last and why some that do are so boring and mundane. Fortunately, God never asks us to do anything which He will not help us accomplish. So, dear husbands, admit your need for God, ask Him to help you, and consider these thoughts.

Real love is not feeling, it is action. As you know, sometimes you have warm feelings of emotion exuding from you to your wife and other times you do not. On the other hand, sometimes you have cold feelings of hostility and resentment flowing from you to her, or from her to you. Prolonged cool feelings are what prompt many couples to conclude they have "fallen out of love." But take heart, as you begin to love her as Christ loved the Church and give yourself for her, there will be fewer periods of cool feelings and more warm and pleasant emotions. Keep this in mind. Feelings are not love, they are the by-products of love.

Consider Christ's greatest display of love—His death on the Cross. Go back to Gethsemane for a minute and try to find the warm emotion of love as He anticipated dying for sinners. I cannot find it. Instead I hear Him asking to be released from His impending agony. But, notice, that Christ went on willingly to die for you and me, exemplifying His own words, "Greater love has no one than this, that one lay down his life for his friends" (John 15:13, NIV).* Thank God Christ did not fall in and out of love with man depending on the way He felt at the time.

Marriage is a lifelong commitment. The mood of our society is to make marriage expedient. That is, marriage is fine if it is meeting everyone's needs and making everyone happy. If it is not, dissolve it. Then, we try to convince ourselves, and everyone else, that everyone is better off because of the divorce—and life goes on as usual. The problem is that no one is better off, and life goes on but we wish it would stop, or go back, or be anything except what it is. Christ's way is so much better. He says a man must not divorce his wife because marriage is for a lifetime (1 Corinthians 7:11). Believing that, we must admonish people considering marriage to weigh their decision very carefully. We must also be sure that those who are married handle their relationship with tender loving care because a lifetime can be a long time. But, there is more. God's intention is that your lifetime of marriage be a meaningful, happy, and good one. The chances that that will happen are greatly improved when Christian husbands willingly give their life for their wife as Christ did for the Church.

In marriage, a man leaves his father and mother and cleaves to his wife. If, when a man marries, he does not "fly the coop," then his parents better "kick him out of the nest," because God has instructed him to leave. Leaving is more than packing your bags and moving your trophies to another house. Someone has said, "Home is where the heart is." Thus it is necessary to move your heart out of your parent's house and into the home you and your wife have established. Usually it comes very naturally. Most of us can remember the bittersweet visit home when we were struck with the realization that it was not our home anymore. We just did not belong because our heart was not there. Wives need visible evidence that their husbands are more husband than son. A husband can demonstrate his independence by his loyalty to his wife. For instance, he will never discuss important matters with his parents before he has talked them over with her. He will never give one of his wife's tasks to his mother to do. You see, wives need to be meeting the important needs of their husbands and then receiving praise and appreciation from him.

Do not be financially dependent on your parents.

Include your wife in your visits to your parents' home and build her up and praise her in their presence.

Be the spiritual leader in your marriage. As a rule, wives are much more responsive, they are much more forgiving when he falters because they know his sincere motive is to go God's way. A husband demonstrates his spiritual sensitivity to his wife by initiating consistent family Bible reading and prayer, by regular church attendance, by reading Christian books, by seeking fellowship with other Christians, and by discussing spiritual goals and achievements with his wife.

Give your wife approval, praise, and admiration. Focus on the positives and the negatives will begin to melt away. Focus on the negatives and the positives will fade into oblivion. Your wife wants to please you and make you appreciate her even more than you want her to. William James has said, "The deepest principle in human nature is the craving to be appreciated." If you do not believe that, try giving your wife sincere praise and admiration for a while and see what happens. She will, probably, blossom into the very wife you felt she never was, but always wanted her to be. Make her happiness a top priority, and God will bless you with the wife of your dreams.

Be intimate with your wife. Intimacy is probably the one thing your wife wants most in marriage. Real intimacy is not physical, though physical intimacy is important in a good marriage and a pleasant by-product of real intimacy. Real intimacy is a oneness of spirit, a deep knowledge of the innermost thoughts and feelings of each other. It is knowing what the other person is going to do even before they do it because you know how they really feel and think. This kind of intimacy is risky because it gives the other person all the weapons needed to hurt you deeply. On the other hand, it provides them with all the tools necessary to meet your deepest needs and heal your secret hurts. Intimacy like that is hard to come by because it takes a lot of planned time together, a true commitment to each other's happiness, and a love that lays down its life for the beloved. Be it ever so expensive, it is a treasure worth the investment.

Finally, **do not place conditions or expectations on your love.** Shakespeare said, "Love sought is good, but given unsought, is better." Christ loved us even when we did not love Him. In fact, the Bible tells us that we love Him because He first loved us. In your marriage, give love, in deeds, to your wife without any thought, or expectation of return, and then the love will flow back to you in wonderful, pleasing ways.

"We are souls living in bodies. Therefore, when we really fall in love, it isn't just physical attraction . . . it's also spiritual attraction. God has opened our eyes and let us see into someone's soul. We have fallen in love with the inner person, the person who is going to live forever. That's why God is the greatest asset to romance. He thought it up in the first place. Include him in every part of your marriage, and he will lift it above the level of the mundane to something rare and beautiful and lasting" (Peter Marshall, from *A Man Called Peter*).

---

*From *The Holy Bible, New International Version*, copyright © 1978 by New York International Bible Society. Used by permission.

Chapter 12

Sex Should Be Fun

by Larry and Nordis Christenson

Background Scriptures: Song of Solomon 4:1-15

We came at our sexual relationship in a fairly uncompli-
cated way. We just expected it would be fun—and it was. Today,
years later, we still think it is one of the best ideas God ever had.

Our culture extols the high pleasure of sex, and no Vic-
torian hush mutes the message. We discovered, however, that
good sex doesn't happen automatically. The pleasure and fulfillment of sex involves more than two people sleeping together
in the same bed. When the sexual relationship in marriage is
left to just happen, it can as easily lead to frustration and disappointment as to satisfaction. The high pleasure of sex is as
much an achievement as it is a discovery.

No advice on the sexual relationship in marriage, we believe, is as practical and profound as two verses in the New
Testament. In 45 words the apostle Paul captures the essence
of an effective sexual relationship. Any couple that will take the
time to understand the simple wisdom of these words will open
the door to an enrichment of their sexual relationship—

The husband should give to his wife her conjugal rights, and likewise the wife to her husband. For the wife does not rule over her own body, but the husband does; likewise the husband does not rule over his own body, but the wife does (1 Corinthians 7:3-4, RSV).

These words bear on three interrelated dynamics of the sexual relationship: *attitude, atmosphere,* and *action.*

Attitude

The apostle's point of departure may at first dismay us: The attitude toward the sexual relationship is formed around the controlling concept of *duty.* Not pleasure, not satisfaction, not rights, but duty.

The apostle recognizes that husband and wife each have marital rights; they have strong urges which need to be satisfied. But this is not what shapes their basic attitude. His word is carefully directed not to the one who has a sexual need, but to the one who has the duty to fulfill it.

The literal meaning in the original Greek is droll: "The husband should pay up on the debt he owes his wife." Some romantic approach! "Well, dear, I managed to scrape together another payment . . ."

Husband and wife are mutually "indebted" to fulfill the

sexual needs of the other. It is interesting to note that in other connections Paul recognizes the headship of the husband and the submission of the wife. But in regard to the sexual relation the submission is mutual: The wife has authority over the husband's body and the husband over the wife's.

This is the attitude which needs to control one's approach to the sexual relationship. My mate has a claim upon me, sexually. It is my duty and my privilege to fulfill that claim.

In order to do this I must have some understanding of her expectations, and she of mine. We need to communicate with each other, tell what we like and what we don't like, what excites us and what leaves us cold.

Our expectations, of course, must be realistic. By this we do not mean that our expectations should be prosaic, dull, or unimaginative. We mean it in the literal sense: Expectations should focus on the real relationship of husband and wife, not on some impossible "ideal" that we carry around subconsciously.

My mate's sexual claim upon me is an *exclusive* claim. The commandment against adultery is more than a negative curb on immorality. It is a positive description of the nature of married love.

An actor, well known for his romantic roles, was asked on a television show what he counsidered essential to being a "great lover." His answer probably surprised the emcee, but it is an answer every husband should engrave in golden letters and hang in his personal hall of wisdom: "A great lover is someone who can satisfy one woman all her life long, and who can be satisfied by one woman all his life long. A great lover isn't someone who goes from woman to woman to woman. Any dog can do that."

It also comes across through fidelity. A husband's and wife's faithfulness to one another undergirds all the other ways they tell each other, "I want you, and no one else. You satisfy me."

This attitude is further enhanced when we recognize the spiritual overtones in the sexual relationship. Marriage symbolizes the love of Christ for His Church, the love of God for

His people (see Ephesians 5:32). That is why Satan hates sex and does everything he can do to pervert it. He knows the authority of symbols in spiritual things. Every time a husband and wife come together in marriage they invoke a powerful symbol of love between God and man, a love which Satan has set himself to destroy.

Atmosphere

Sex is a drama. In a drama the actors move through a series of events toward the destiny or climax envisioned for them by the playwright. The divine Playwright has set before husband and wife the destiny to become one (Genesis 2:24; see also Matthew 19:3-6; Ephesians 5:28-32). The sexual encounter is a drama in which they fulfill their God-appointed destiny.

By "right atmosphere" we are not suggesting a universal norm. The right atmosphere is the one that is right for a particular couple at a particular time. Most of us, however, could afford to be more imaginative in creating atmosphere for the sexual encounter.

We suggest three basic ingredients that contribute to atmosphere. They can be mixed together with as much variety and innovation as a couple wants: *service, suspense,* and *setting.*

Service

This has to do with the overall atmosphere in the home, the broad "backdrop" for the sexual drama. How do you relate to each other in the normal happenings of married life? How do you speak to one another in the day-to-day routine? A poor scene in the bedroom at 9:30 p.m. may trace back to a thoughtless remark over breakfast coffee.

A frequent complaint voiced by wives goes something like this: "All my husband is interested in is sex." When you pursue that complaint, you discover that usually it does not mean that the wife is uninterested in sex. In some cases she may actually have a stronger sexual appetite than her husband. What the complaint really means is, "I don't like it when the only personal attention I get from my husband is in bed. I want to be more than a sex object."

A woman's sexuality is more diffuse than a man's. For her the atmosphere that supports the sexual encounter must extend beyond the bedroom. She needs to feel herself encircled by her husband's care and commitment in order fully to abandon herself to his sexual embrace.

Suspense

Like any drama, the drama of sex is heightened when an element of suspense is added.

Many people equate suspense with uncertainty: Suspense is "not knowing what is going to happen next." But in order to have suspense you must focus the uncertainty by introducing a clear note of prediction or intention. You must tell what is going to happen, or what someone intends to do. That is what creates suspense.

A man who kisses his wife good-bye and says, "Have a nice day," does not create much suspense.

A husband who lets his wife know that he desires her, and intimates his intentions, injects a note of anticipation and suspense into the atmosphere.

"Tonight after dinner I'm going to take the phone off the hook."

"You are?"

"Yes. And then I'm going to build a roaring fire in the fireplace. And I'm going to stretch out on that nice new carpet and watch the flames dance in your eyes."

"You'll have to get close in order to see them."

"I'm going to."

"And if I close my eyes?"

"Then I'll get closer still . . ."

Sometimes, when husband and wife sense a desire for each other, but the time or situation does not allow it, a promise of "tonight . . ." or "when I get back . . ." can add a winsome expectancy to the atmosphere. If a man is away from home, he can introduce an element of anticipation by something he writes in a letter.

100

Of couse the sexual encounter is often delightful when it is spontaneous and unplanned. But both husband and wife can afford to vary this by bringing in an element of suspense from time to time. Anticipation adds a particular kind of enjoyment to the sexual relationship. It can also help the woman, whose sexual arousal is slower and more subtle than the man's, come to the encounter more eager and responsive.

Setting

The most common setting for the sexual encounter is (a) at night, (b) in bed. It is the time and the place most convenient and natural for most couples.

Slight changes in this standard setting can enhance the encounter. You might experiment with the lighting. Making love in the dark heightens the sense of touch. But the encounter can also be enhanced by visual stimulation. One man said that he and his wife especially enjoyed making love by candlelight.

What you wear is also part of the setting, and can be varied, sometimes with startling effect. One woman, at the suggestion of a marriage counselor, came into the bedroom wearing a fur coat and high heels—and nothing else. Her husband was already in his pajamas, sitting on the edge of the bed.

"What's up?" he asked innocently. "Aren't you coming to bed?"

"I am," she said, slipping out of her heels as she walked toward him.

The next morning as he was leaving for work he said, "Hey, that fur coat routine—that was something else!" A week later *he* came into the bedroom—dressed like a pirate!

They both concluded that their sexual relationship had become dull, and these little episodes helped to lighten the atmosphere.

"At first I thought it was silly," the wife said, "but we both enjoyed it, so who cares?"

That is the essential criterion: Do both husband and wife enjoy it? Does it add to their sense of fun and pleasure? Does it refresh the relationship?

The standard setting may be perfectly satisfactory most of

the time. But from time to time you will both enjoy a touch of variety. A different time of day. A different place. A provocative nightgown.

One last word about the setting. It must be *securely private.* The wife, especially, cannot abandon herself to the sexual encounter if she fears being intruded upon. A lock on the bedroom door is a wise investment for successful sex.

Action

Traditionally men have been regarded as "active" in the sexual relationship, women as "passive." Current Christian literature on sex is fairly consistent in urging the wife to take a more active role in the relationship. A survey of 100,000 women by *Redbook* magazine indicated that women, especially those who consider themselves "religious," are active partners in the sexual relationship. This is a wholesome corrective of the image of a wife as a passive, silently enduring martyr.

There is a sense, however, in which the traditional roles are still helpful in understanding the dynamics of the sexual relationship. The *Redbook* survey indicated that even though wives are active partners in the relationship, the sexual encounter is still *initiated* by husbands the majority of the time. Our own research, which included both husbands and wives, indicated this even more strongly. This appears to be true in all age brackets and simply reflects a universal characteristic of the man-woman relationship: The man is usually the initiator, the woman the responder.

Putting these two factors together, we could describe the woman's participation as *actively passive,* i.e., she is an *active responder.*

In her book, *The Total Woman,* Marabel Morgan writes, "A woman's hands should never be still when she is making love. By caressing tenderly, you assure him that he's touchable. Tell him 'I love you' with your hands." That's a good picture of an active responder.

The man, on the other hand, could be described as *passively active,* i.e., he is a *responsive initiator.* As the lovemaking gets under way, he must be sensitive to his wife's needs and desires. He must key his actions to her rising response.

Successful sex depends in considerable measure on how willing husband and wife are to instruct one another.

Kay Arthur, popular lecturer on the marriage relationship, said in one of her talks, "When you go to bed with your husband, make sure you enjoy it. Don't just lie there and endure. Make it fun. It's important for your husband to know that he satisfies you. That's why you have to share with him *how* to satisfy you."

In a survey we conducted, one thing we suggested was for husband and wife each to write a brief scenario "in which you tell your mate exactly how you would like to experience an act of loveplay and intercourse, giving specific instructions as to what would make it enjoyable for you."

Some couples find it more difficult than others to verbalize their ideas and desires. That does not mean they cannot instruct one another. The communication that takes place during the sexual encounter, much of it non-verbal, can gently direct the mate to do those things that please and satisfy—sighs, whispers, guiding the hands, bodily movements. However it is communicated, husbands and wives need to let each other know exactly what they want. Only in this way can they do what they are committed to do, and what each deeply wants to do, and that is truly to serve one another, to bring the mate to the point of complete sexual fulfillment and satisfaction.

Reprinted by permission from *The Christian Couple,* by Larry and Nordis Christenson, published and copyright 1977, Bethany Fellowship, Inc., Minneapolis, MN 55438.

Chapter 13

Developing a Strong Spiritual Life Together

by Phyllis and Randy Michael

Background Scriptures: John 14:16-17, 26-27;
1 Corinthians 12:12-26

Preface: We have elected to write in a testimonial style. We hope that such a style will prove to be helpful. In addition, we have divided our assignment into two sections, Phyllis writing the first and Randy, the second. However, we dialogued the entire chapter first.

Part I: Our Pilgrimage

We looked at each other in frustration and discouragement. Another week had gone by and we still had not had "family devotions." I felt guilty and condemned. How could God be pleased with us—a pastor and wife unable to find time reading together, and praying, but these times seemed so outlined. Interruptions or unexpected schedule changes often short-circuited our well-laid plans. The result: guilt feelings. Those little signs, "Ours Is a Family Altar Home," only added to my frustration. I had visions of everyone else happily gathered in loving, warm, family groups every day, and having family devotions while Randy and I remained spasmodic in our attempts.

How surprising, then, it was to hear another Christian wife and mother whom I admired say, "Family devotions are a real problem to us in our home." Could it be true? Were others also struggling with this issue in their marriages? As the years have passed, I have realized that not only were we not alone, we were surrounded by Christian couples wanting to share spiritual life together, but not knowing how.

And the guilt? Well, Satan must take credit for using our unreal expectations and faulty images of what spiritual life together would mean. God lovingly draws us to himself; Satan condemns us when we don't "measure up," whether the standard is real or not.

Pain and difficulty in the area of shared spiritual life have allowed us first to admit we had a need and then have motivated us to find God's solution.

In the early years of our marriage, when frustration and guilt were so prevalent, I did not realize that while not possessing the total answer to the "family devotions" issue, Randy and I were on the way to deep satisfaction in this area. We were individually discovering the joy of spending quality time with God and His Word. I had, since childhood, read the Bible with some regularity—"a chapter a day keeps the devil away," or so I thought, but I really did not know what it meant to "abide in Him." I was hungry for a deeper spiritual walk. Randy came to know the Lord at 16 and began his Christian life by meditating on God's Word. When we married, he already had a regular habit of saturating himself with the Word. As I observed him and as he shared with me what God's Word meant in his personal devotional life, I began to try his method. What a difference! The pattern is deceptively simple and yet profoundly significant. I would read a short portion of scripture, perhaps a few verses from a book like Ephesians, and ask the Lord to open up His message for me that day. I would then praise Him for the content of the reading. For example, Ephesians 2:4-7 says this:

But God, being rich in mercy, because of His great love with which He loved us, even when we were dead in our transgressions, made us alive together with Christ (by grace you have been saved), and raised us up with Him, and seated us with Him in the heavenly places, in Christ Jesus, in order that in the ages to come He might show the surpassing riches of His grace in kindness toward us in Christ Jesus (NASB).*

Often I read until I come to a period signaling the end of one thought. "Thank You, Lord, for Your rich mercy and great love. Thank You, that even when I was dead in sin, You made me alive. Thank You, that You have done all this to be kind to me forever and forever."

Next, I would confess an inner need in relation to the verse passage I had read. "Lord, I need Your help to comprehend what You've done for me. Sometimes I'm ungrateful and forget to praise You. Last night, I had an inner attitude of bitterness toward You because of hurt feelings. Forgive me." After a time of openness and confession before Him I would pray and ask for answers to specific needs on the basis of the passage. "Lord, we need Your help. You are rich and gracious. We need Your help financially right now. There is a debt that needs paying and we don't have the funds. Supply our need in Your own way and time." Then I would close with another time of thanking Him for what He would do in the future.

There are other methods of spending time with His Word personally that Randy and I have both employed. All of them focus on meditating on the gracious kindness of God revealed through His Word. We have enjoyed the "SMU" approach to a passage, "What does it say?" "What does it mean?" and "How can I use it?" Also, we have written our responses to God and our lives while studying His Word. Memorizing verses that really speak to us has also been helpful. Whatever the specific process used, I believe personal devotions are most productive when centered directly on the Bible and its application to everyday life. I have found that a personal time with the Lord is something I now eagerly anticipate.

Gradually, as we continued to individually grow in response to our private times with the Lord, we spontaneously told each other of our pilgrimages. Often, we would linger at the breakfast table and just talk about what we had discovered recently about ourselves and our relationship to God, and others. We would pray together about our discoveries or needs in relation to the Word. We began to realize that indeed we were sharing a spiritual life together. It was not something imposed by guilt or "shoulds" or "oughts." It came from the overflow of God's work in each of us.

At that point we learned that we could establish a pattern that worked for us. As we have told other married couples about this pattern, they have responded with enthusiasm. Usually, we set aside three or four times a week. For us, it has been helpful to plan the week ahead on Sunday afternoon. We mark on our calendars specific times for spiritual sharing, knowing that our planning is flexible.

A typical time will be after lunch. Randy's office in the home makes this possible. Here is what might happen:

Randy: "Phyl, I was reading last night in Second Corinthians and 6:10 really hit me. Paul was describing himself in these ways, '. . . as sorrowful yet always rejoicing, as poor yet making many rich, as having nothing and yet possessing all things' (NASB). As I thought about this, the Lord spoke to me that the paradox of this verse is descriptive of our life right now. We're not circumstantially all that well off, and yet we are able to minister to others and 'make them rich' in personal and interpersonal growth. How do you relate to that?"

After each of us shares our discoveries from a particular passage, we then talk together (dialogue) about the implications of the verses for us. Often we will pray together about what we have found in the Word as it relates to our needs. Finally, we make some commitment to action on the basis of the Word. Many times we experience a closeness during our sharing that spreads into other areas of our relationship. Our spirits commune and we experience a sense of our potential as a Christian couple.

> Together we are helped
> healed
> strengthened
> united.

God has indeed allowed us to know the truth of Colossians 3:16-17. "Let the word of Christ richly dwell within you . . . giving thanks to God the Father" (NASB).

Part II: Some of the Fruit

In physics, a law states that when two objects draw closer to a third object, they are closer to one another. So it is when two marriage partners seek the Lord they discover they either can be, or are, closer to one another.

Phyllis has explained our "method" of drawing closer to the Lord and hence to one another. I want to tell you some of the fruit of this "drawing closer."

The first: self-awareness. The writer to the Hebrews declares that God's Word can discern the thoughts and intentions of our hearts (cf. Hebrews 4:12). I need that. I may not always want it, but I need it. We are limited by our own perspectives, inclinations, and biases, and yet not always aware of our limitations. Marital studies show that one very important requisite for a growing marriage is each partner's self-awareness of his or her strengths and weaknesses. My pursuit of God has helped me become more self-aware. He knows me; He knows what is in me (cf. Psalm 139:1-6). He reveals himself and myself to me.

At times He relates to me as an "affirmer," helping me to be aware of my strengths, gifts, abilities, and positive ways of relating. At other times He relates to me as "conviction," not in the sense of negative, judgmental accusing, but as One who points out something to help me. He believes in me, thus He is honest with me. He helps me to be aware of how I am relating to my partner, and I need that, too.

The second yield: an awareness and valuing of my partner. Again, marital studies have shown that awareness of and valuing (esteeming) one's partner are crucial for marital satisfaction. As I work with couples, I find two intermingled dynamics. On the one hand, there is a tendency toward awareness of the partner without an awareness of self. This is often seen in accusing, blaming, and playing the game "If only . . ." ("If only you would do such and such, then our marriage or I could be such and such.") The awareness of partner at this point is usually focused only on the partner's shortcomings and not on his or her strengths. Further, the "awareness" is usually a distorted one, out of focus, because of the build-up of negative feeling in the "observing" partner. When I speak of the awareness of partner that God has helped me have, I am speaking of being aware of my partner's strengths and "weaknesses" and valuing her as a person of worth. With the Lord's help, I seek to compliment her on her strengths and complement her in regard to her "lesser strengths."

On the other hand, I see partners who are only aware of self and not their partner. They do not see or value or hear their partner as a person, or the qualities the partner has. They tend to be aware only of their own feelings, interests, longings, and hurts. The irony is that although they are more aware of self or are only aware of self, they are not really self-aware. They do not see that their view is myopic. Further, they do not see their own shortcomings. They may talk of having some but they cannot name them and/or they do not "own" them and particularly they do not try to modify them. However, I must not limit this description to "couples I work with"—I have these tendencies myself! But, God has helped me be aware of these tendencies and to deal with them.

A third fruit: commitment. A study done by a major university reveals that a lifetime commitment to one another as marriage partners is a determining factor in marital success. This should not surprise the Christian, but it is good to have studies like this that substantiate God's pattern for marriage. As a human being, I have times when I want to give up, not just in marriage but in all of life. Demands and difficulties build up and the fantasies of quitting dance in my mind. I can see myself as a ski bum in the winter and a backpacker in the summer. These may not be viable options, only fleeting, "release valves," but increasingly people are quitting relationships, trading in the "used" one for a "new" one. However, God has helped me be committed to my partner for life, not just until the first problem or disagreement, or even the fifth or five-hundredth.

Personally, God has grounded us in a reality beyond ourselves and this has given us a sense of commitment to Him and to one another. Rather than being negative, this has been a positive, stabilizing factor for us when patience has been short and marital excitement has been at low ebb. I think of Paul's admonition to the Galatians, "And let us not lose heart in doing good, for in due time we shall reap if we do not grow weary" (6:9). The result of the commitment has always been, sooner or later, a continuing or increased sense of fulfillment and belonging, intimacy, and security. We have reaped a harvest and will continue to have an ever greater harvest.

A fourth yield: "a harvest" of warmth, closeness, and especially, intimacy. God has helped us open ourselves to ourselves and to one another. I think of Adam and Eve in the Garden after they had sinned. They became aware that they were naked and sewed fig leaves together for clothing. From whom did the clothing hide them? Not from God! There is within us both a desire for intimacy and a fear of it.

Our personal relationship with God has helped us take off the inadequate ways we clothe ourselves to hide ourselves from each other and to share ourselves with each other. It has not always been easy, but I have found in my times of candidness about my inner struggles, hesitancies, and feelings that my partner has been perceptive, supportive, caring, and kind. We have found that for the sharing one it was a great struggle at first. "What will the partner think? Will he/she ridicule? Will he/she not listen? Just what will he/she do?" We have found that the struggle is more inside the one sharing than the one listening. In our experience, the other partner has never ridiculed a candid self-disclosure. There has been an intense listening and the revelations have never been disclosed outside the marital pair. The result has been a greater knowledge of each other and, therefore, more tenderness, appreciation, and respect.

A fifth result: a motivation that transcends our human powers. God has greatly endowed mankind with intelligence, creativity, ability to envision and to empathize, but there are times in marriage when great internal forces almost entirely envelop me and with great power draw me away from what would be useful, constructive, and loving. At those times it seems almost impossible to say,

"I'm sorry."

"I was wrong; will you please forgive me?"

"Hey, that was in poor taste—I'll work on it!"

Only a few words, right? But life pivots on them. I have found God helps me; He provides a motivation to say them, and increasingly mean those words that are so hard to say. It may take me a little while but He is persistent and eventually I am able to say them.

Together we are discovering the adventure of sharing deeply in the things of the Lord and in each other's lives. Our journey this far has not been easy but it is increasingly rewarding. We have not settled down to mediocrity, but we are geared up for growth together!

*From the *New American Standard Bible,* © The Lockman Foundation, 1960, 1962, 1968, 1971, 1972, 1973, 1975. Used by permission.